John Howard Cowperthwait

Money, Silver, and Finance

John Howard Cowperthwait

Money, Silver, and Finance

ISBN/EAN: 9783743320505

Manufactured in Europe, USA, Canada, Australia, Japa

Cover: Foto ©ninafisch / pixelio.de

Manufactured and distributed by brebook publishing software (www.brebook.com)

John Howard Cowperthwait

Money, Silver, and Finance

PREFACE TO THE FIRST EDITION.

The author presumes that a business man may be pardoned for writing upon a business question, when that question is paramount in public importance.

He has tried to answer The Silver Question by arguments based both upon the truths of financial science and upon the principles which underlie the operation of what is called business. And, admitting shortcomings, he ventures to hope that a student in finance may find in this volume a sought-for portrayal of business ways; that a busy man of affairs may find herein some scientific points which may have hitherto escaped his attention; or, that a few of the readers of this book will be compensated for their trouble by the fastening more firmly together of the links in their own chain of evidence against silver fallacies. The author's position may be that of a distributer of ideas, rather than that of a producer; and he will make no complaint if he be called a mere retailer, who simply does his best to display the product of others in that manner which his judgment tells him, truly or not, may suit the general public.

The first chapter herein appeared originally in *Lippincott's Magazine:* and the subject-matter of an essay, written for *The Engineering and Mining Journal,* has been divided for using now a second time. Many newspapers kindly reproduced these articles wholly or in part.

Sufficient excuse for the publication of a book of this character is thought to lie in these facts: The Senate of the United States, Fifty-first Congress, passed a free-coinage measure; the House came near agreeing to this measure; the Fifty-second Congress was elected at the time when the "silver craze" was said to be in possession of the wits of the people; and now prominent men in and out of Congress, and influential journals, are advocating energetically, the policy of free silver coinage, or unlimited silver purchase.

* * * * * *

BROOKLYN, N. Y., January, 1892.

PREFACE TO THE THIRD EDITION.

The events of the four years which have elapsed since this work was written have not made absolutely necessary any changes in the arguments used. While it is true that the purchasing clause of the Silver Purchase Law has been repealed, and thereby one of the targets of this book removed, yet it is also true that the free-coinage movement of to-day still commands the vote of a majority of the Senate of the United States and the influence of prominent men and journals, particularly in the West and the South. Asking the reader to bear in mind that the United States no longer buys silver bullion, the author feels justified in thinking that it may be better to leave the arguments as originally put forth, for if they possessed any value at that time, they should now possess a greater value, the price of silver bullion having continued to decline, as predicted, the production of gold having grown to the vast sum of $200,000,000 worth per annum, and the world's stock of available gold having largely increased.

Foot-notes have been freely introduced.

Recent financial events are treated in a new concluding chapter. There the author has taken the opportunity for giving his views on the Panic of 1893, revenue deficiency, bond-issuing, redundancy, the circulation, bi-metallism, and the present financial situation. Reasons are given also for placing the cause of Sound Money first in the coming election, even to the exclusion of all other causes.

NEW YORK, May, 1896.

PREFACE TO THE FIFTH EDITION.

PUBLIC Opinion has decreed that the Election of 1896 shall settle the Currency Question. In spite of protests, tardy politicians are being swept into either the Gold Camp or the Silver Camp. Bi-metallism is no longer a good fence to perch upon, and Protection is no longer a barrier against inquiries on the all-absorbing issue.

The Republican chieftain, with hands outstretched for a Protection banner, has been told to carry the Gold Standard. Two-thirds of the Democratic braves have lashed out of their camp an obstinate third, so that the regular Democracy, this year, shall stand for Silver only.

The Silver Party has an advantage in promptly awakening enthusiasm by claiming to be able to right an alleged wrong, and to rescue all who suffer from it—the alleged "Crime of 1873."

The author is sure, however, that a vast majority of the American people will be found on the right side in the final contest, if every day of the hundred intervening days be put to the best uses. Within this short time millions of voters must be taught the truths of financial and monetary science.

NEW YORK, July, 1896.

CONTENTS.

	PAGE
PREFACE	iii

CHAPTER
- I.—THE EVOLUTION OF MONEY, TRADE, AND FINANCE 1
- II.—THE MOVEMENTS OF PRICES . . 23
- III.—INDIA AND HER SILVER RUPEE . . 49
- IV.—PRICES AND WAGES 62
- V.—PRICES, WAGES, AND LABOR-SAVING MACHINERY 80
- VI.—"THE DEBTOR CLASS" . . . 101
- VII.—"THE BALANCE OF TRADE"—FOREIGN EXCHANGE 114
- VIII.—FOREIGN EXCHANGE UNDER NORMAL AND UNDER ABNORMAL CONDITIONS, 132
- IX.—DISCUSSION WITH REPRESENTATIVE ADVOCATES OF SILVER . . . 144
- X.—THE DISCUSSION CONCLUDED . . 158
- XI.—"ULTIMATE REDEMPTION" . . 175
- XII.—THE OLD VOLUME-OF-MONEY THEORY, 183
- XIII.—SUPPLEMENTAL—A RETROSPECT—THE PANIC OF 1893—REVENUE DEFICIENCY—FINANCIAL FLOUNDERING—BOND-ISSUING—PAPER MONEY REDUNDANCY—THE CIRCULATION—BI-METALLISM—THE FINANCIAL SITUATION IN 1896—THE ELECTION—CONCLUSION 202

MONEY, SILVER, AND FINANCE.

CHAPTER I.

THE EVOLUTION OF MONEY, TRADE, AND FINANCE.

In the dawn of trade and civilization—and I mention trade first because civilization has been supported by trade, although sometimes affecting to despise it—there arose a necessity for money, and different communities groped about until each found its most available substance. Adam Smith tells us that in the rude ages of society cattle were the common instrument of commerce, the armor of Diomede, according to Homer, costing nine oxen, while that of Glaucus cost a hundred. Salt has been used as money in Abyssinia; a species of shells (cowries) in some parts of the coast of

India; dried cod in Newfoundland; tobacco in Virginia; sugar in the West Indies; hides, leather, furs, etc., elsewhere. Circumstances too have forced the use of inferior money upon people who had grown accustomed to better; for instance, our colonists along the coasts of Long Island Sound adopted the money of the Indians and made wampum (polished beads made of parts of the periwinkle and the clam-shell) a legal tender for sums up to twelvepence, and, by custom, made it the prevailing currency. The superiority of the white man was shown, however, by his ability to counterfeit this wampum, as Professor Sumner dryly mentions in his *History of American Currency*.

It is a long way from the many articles named, and from the irregular pieces of metal which almost everywhere superseded them, to a five-dollar gold piece, a twenty-five-cent silver piece, a nickel five-cent piece, and a bronze or copper cent, or to a Bank-of-England five-pound note, and the car of progress has frequently tumbled into a paper-concealed ditch; but comparatively perfect forms of money and its substitutes have at length been evolved, and the whole process by which copper, bronze, nickel, silver, gold, and paper have taken relative positions has been strictly evolutionary, the actions of governments having been forced upon them by irresistible natural law. Copper, bronze, and nickel have proved their suitability for small change and their unsuitability for large coinage. Silver has proved its suitability for dimes, quarters, and half-dollars and its unsuitability for dollars or certainly for any larger coin. Gold has proved its unsuitability for smaller coins than quarter- or half-eagles; and, for the ordinary use of money, from hand to hand, gold has been proved inferior to paper. But gold has taken the position of a base for paper money and for national and international exchange of commodities.

The displacement of silver by gold, as a standard measure of value among the great commercial nations, has been as truly evolutionary as has been the displacement, as money, of unsuitable articles: the important cause was the cheapening of silver through over-production and through a natural decline in the cost of production. Supply exceeded demand, at or near current prices. About the year 1873, silver became so plentiful in the United States that it began to circulate side by side with paper money, although gold was then at a premium of say ten per cent. In Europe, the cheapening of silver was helped on by the belief of individual governments that silver would displace gold in that country which should continue to largely coin silver,—Gresham's Law,[1] the economic law under which an inferior kind of money tends to drive from a country a superior kind of money, being well understood over there. It was seen that if a large quantity of silver were coined, after its bullion value had declined, gold coins might be melted down and then sold by weight. It is said that Germany thought it a good time to put its money upon a safe gold basis and to force France to drift upon the silver basis. Then too, a government which should be the quickest to reduce

[1] Discovered by Sir Thomas Gresham (1519–1579).

the quantity of its silver coin in circulation, therefore the quickest to make room for gold to circulate, might succeed in attracting gold from other countries. England, of course, could not afford to be behindhand, for bills of exchange are drawn upon London in all quarters of the globe, and every one of these bills is payable in gold, the commercial supremacy of England, indeed, depending upon the world's belief that she has sufficient gold to meet all possible demands, and upon the world's knowledge that the note of the Bank of England has commanded gold for three quarters of a century. The pathetic view of the actions of European governments in stopping the coining of silver, prompted by fear that a continuance of silver-coining might lead to the actual demonetization of gold may be found in the minority report of the Committee on Coinage, Weights, and Measures, on the Senate Silver Bill, second session, Fifty-first Congress. Silver might have maintained its parity with gold if nobody had given silver a kick, thinking it would go down anyway; just as a failed bank might not have succumbed if nobody had started a rumor as to its solvency and no depositor had been mean enough to start "a run."

The fluctuating and declining value of silver during the past twenty years, and the fear that an unlimited quantity might or may be produced, coupled with the stability of gold during the period since the discovery of the Californian supply,[1] and the belief that all gold-mines, together, cannot be sufficiently prolific to affect the value of gold, have made gold the standard of value for great commercial nations, and have served to fasten silver upon the weaker commercial nations as their standard of value. If a country trading with England or the United States would take silver it would be sure to get it, for everybody pays debts with as cheap money as creditors will take. If a country persisted in coining gold, and in refusing to coin silver, that country could not have any other country's surplus of silver dumped upon it. Possessing inexhaustible mines of silver, we favor the use of this metal as a standard of

[1] And, later, the South African supply.

value; but it cannot be to our interest to lose sight of the fact that silver is already discredited by the commercial world,—not merely by governments, some of which might be induced to change, but by commerce itself, which selects for itself the best standard of value. As well say to the world, We have plenty of wood in this country, we will build a wooden navy, and then you will discard iron-clads; or, We will give up using electricity, and then you will go back to steam and to candles and oil; as well take such a position, as to say that the world would follow our example if we should abandon gold and fully adopt silver for our standard of value. Evolution is as irresistible in the financial and commercial world as everywhere else; evolution has selected gold, and has rejected silver; and all we can do in the matter is to decide whether we shall take as our standard the selected metal or the rejected metal,—that is, stand with the great nations or with the weak nations. Wampum was perfect money for the Indians, and was a fair sort for the colonists, but was of no use in foreign commerce. Wampum cost time and labor to produce, but Europe did not want it; and arguments to prove to Europeans their own perversity fall about equally flat whether in favor of wampum or of silver, excepting, of course, that Europe wants some silver, whereas it never wanted any wampum. Two facts overcome all arguments; the production of silver has too largely increased, and the price of silver has too greatly declined.

Statistics show how naturally silver has lost caste as a standard of value. Up to 1870 the world's annual production was less than half so great as the annual production of gold (coinage value), and therefore the price of silver was above one dollar and thirty cents per ounce, the parity of the two metals being close to fifteen and one half ounces of silver to one ounce of gold. But while the average production of gold has not materially changed,[1] that of silver has so largely increased that it is now

[1] NOTE TO FOURTH EDITION.—See table on page 160 and also the foot note.

about one third greater than the production of gold. There are grounds for believing, too, that gold will be still further distanced. Under the circumstances, the supply of silver far outrunning the demand, it is not unnatural that silver should be worth, to-day, less than one dollar per ounce, and that the ratio of value should be about twenty-one or twenty-two to one. Sixteen to one is the United States coinage parity, corresponding with $1.2929 per ounce for silver,—say thirty per cent. above the world's price.[1]

Trade and civilization could hardly have developed beyond a primitive state before the business of banking must have come into existence, crude, but essentially similar to modern banking, the intricacies of to-day's financial operations corresponding to the intricacies of to-day's trade. And as a large portion of the inhabitants of the globe would have frozen or have starved, or never would have come into being, if the world had not learned to use money, simple barter being wholly inadequate to perform the smallest fraction of the ex-

[1] In 1896 the price of silver is about sixty-eight cents per ounce, the market value ratio to gold being about 31 to 1.

change of products, so financial **systems are absolutely** necessary to **the business of the present time, the world's population now largely** depending **for the** continuance of its existence upon **the** success of the schemes of dead and living financiers. In **other** words, the needs of the world outstripped the greatest volume of exchanges possible by barter, next the greatest volume possible by both **barter** and the use of money, **and** now, apparently, the volume of exchanges **is limited by** the degree of perfection attained in financial science, transportation problems being often only financial problems.

The ancient planters of rice and **wheat must have been** short of money while their crops were growing, for then the planters would have been obliged to support their hands while receiving nothing; at and before harvest-time a **money-lender** must have been as useful as a banker of our day, who annually sends money westward, "to move **the crops**"; and immediately after the selling **of a crop** the ancient producers would **have been** in position to lend their surplus of money, for the sake of interest. The dealers in rice, wheat, or other produce would need to borrow money when purchasing a crop, and would have money to lend after the crop had been marketed. Raiders or traders, when starting upon an expedition, would need plenty of ready money, and upon their return might find it more profitable to borrow against a heavy stock of ivory than to sell it at once. The weak or timid persons in a primitive community would like to deposit a portion of their savings in the hands of a strong and trustworthy man, especially if such a man would pay something for the use of the money. A rich, strong, trustworthy man, either old or willing to lead a quiet life, would drift into the banking business for power, profit, honor, or simply to oblige his friends and neighbors. Indeed, so naturally does the banking business come up that, without offering further proof, we may assume that this business has been necessary in all the steps of trade and civilization. Certainly it is so necessary in our modern world that wherever we find a large village which has no bank or banker, nor one in proximity, we are pretty sure to find a community that is both poor and ignorant.

Of tremendous importance for good and evil has been and is the financial contrivance which we know as paper money; properly, a receipt for real money and a promise to pay it back on demand. When one person saw fit to trust another with money or other valuable thing, either for safe-keeping or both safe-keeping and interest, the first person would be glad to have a receipt. And if the banker were well known, his receipt might be passed by the first person to a second, in exchange for merchandise. But the first person would want probably a number of things, belonging to a number of people, and not want all the things at once; and he would therefore ask the banker for a number of receipts, each for a convenient portion of the whole deposit. And, as business grew, the banker, for his own convenience, would keep in readiness a great number of receipts, for small and large amounts—that is to say, he would be ready to issue to the public paper money, in small and large denominations. People like paper money because of its lack of weight; but the benefit to the issuer comes only in issuing an amount which exceeds the sum of real money that is supposed to be represented. If a banker issue one hundred thousand dollars in paper money in receipt for one hundred thousand dollars in real money, and keep the real money in his vault, no profit can result. But if he lend seventy-five thousand dollars of the real money on interest, trusting that the public will not demand payment for more than twenty-five thousand dollars of his paper, his profit becomes quite clear; and it is equally clear that the community has the use of a circulating medium seventy-five thousand dollars greater than before. Given the good faith of the issuer, the question whether paper money be a blessing or a curse must always have been mainly a question of quantity, not of exact but of relative quantity,—relative to the real money in the vaults of the issuer, relative to the customs of the public in the matter of carrying money, relative to the public's belief in the wealth back of the issuer, relative to the state of trade, present and prospective and foreign and domestic, relative to the probability or improbability of happenings which, in a moment, would change confidence into panic and bring to the doors of the issuer the holders of most of his paper, crying loudly for gold. In truth, the line between safety and danger in a volume of paper money moves forward and backward with changing circumstances, and holders have always been willing to hold when they thought they were not obliged to hold, and have always demanded payment when they thought that payment might be refused.

When governments took to themselves the right to issue paper money, the drawing of a danger line became still more difficult, because of a prevailing notion that the value of money rests in the governmental stamp upon it. Governments have put forth excessive volumes without knowing that there was any danger, and with an ease which has been equalled only by the difficulty of subsequent withdrawals. Whether given a legal-tender character or not, paper money paid to troops, for food, clothing, weapons, ammunition, or for other things, readily finds its way into circulation. And with a large quantity flowing from the national treasury, people appear to be prosperous, demagogues applaud, and safety is already well behind before any exportation or any hoarding of gold acts as a danger signal. The test of relative quantity applies to government notes as well as to bank-notes; but the former have the advantage of being known by the whole instead of by sections of a community. It is important that A, in the East, trading with B, in the West, should agree to give or take the kind of money that B has in mind; or, for example, that C, in the South, trading with D, in the North, should not be compelled to receive bank-notes which are bankable only in the North, or be permitted to settle a debt with the bank-notes which are bankable only in his own section. Governmental safeguard, guaranty, or responsibility is better than the individual responsibility of widely separated banks and bankers; but whether our present paper money is better than would be paper money which might, under proper supervision, be issued, as proposed by Edward Atkinson, by the New York Clearing-House Association and by other aggregations of banks and bankers, is another question. Such paper money might be changed in volume from time to time, to conform to the natural changes in the state of trade and commerce; and if the issuers were given the right to raise and lower the rate of interest, somewhat as the Bank of England moves its rate, they would possibly be able to give us better paper money, because elastic in volume, than we now possess. I do not think, however, that any new kind of paper money need be recommended in this volume.

Vastly more important to the commercial world than paper money are the other financial contrivances called checks, drafts, notes, bills of exchange, etc.; for, besides having no appreciable weight, they can be made safe in transmission. So used to these substitutes for money has trade grown that millions of people, every day, agree to receive or pay money without thinking of any money more real than one of these substitutes, and without stopping to consider that should one tenth of the traders carry out their contracts literally the other nine tenths would necessarily fail to carry out theirs. But this is far from being an unfortunate thing: it is but a fact in evidence that the volume of exchanges of the world's commodities is so great that money does not suffice for a tenth of the movement; while, of course, it is true that the greater the facilities for moving the world's commodities, the better for everybody. Banks and individuals depend for their solvency upon the willingness, practically, of everybody to forego his rights; but to find fault with this is equivalent to finding fault with the growth of trade. If consumers of American oil, cottons, and hardware in remote parts of the world should send us money to pay for our goods; if British purchasers of American stocks, bonds, wheat, cotton, meat, should pay us actual money; if American buyers of silk should send money to France, or American buyers of coffee and rubber should send money to Brazil; if New York buyers of provisions should send money to Western producers, and Western consumers of manufactured articles send money to Eastern manufacturers,—the bulk of the world's money would always be in transit. And this is equivalent to saying that the exchanges of the world's commodities would not take place,—that we should be in that state of barbarism in which each country uses only its own productions.

In one breath we may fairly speak of the evolution of money, of trade, of finance, and of civilization; for evolution in each has been dependent upon the other three; and to-day fair tests of the state of civilization in any country are the kind of money which it uses, the development of its trade, and the condition and extent of its banking or credit system. Silver is the money of India and China, and we find in those countries that the people are poor and ignorant—so poor that famines recur, that the average weekly wage is not an inconveniently heavy weight of this metal, and that the average amount in people's pockets is not likely to burst them; so ignorant that pieces of paper could hardly be expected to pass from hand to hand like real money; so ignorant that the foreign trade of these countries is conducted mostly by foreigners on the coasts, foreigners alone understanding how to use banking facilities. Exactly opposite is the development reached in the United States: paper money, whether, on its face, redeemable in "gold," in "coin," or in "silver," is preferred to the intrinsically valuable metals, and the paper money, which is redeemable in "dollars," circulates alongside those "dollars" which have been given a legal-tender character; our people are so well off that pocket-money would be burdensome if it were all in silver; the average weekly wage-rate is too great to be paid in silver, if the convenience of either employers or employees is to be considered; and we have in this country such a highly developed system of banking and credit that nearly all of the exchange of commodities among ourselves, and between us and foreigners, is done without more than a nominal use of money. England forces gold and silver to circulate in England by not permitting the people to have paper money in denominations below five pounds—say twenty-five dollars,—and France forces Frenchmen to use gold and silver by not giving Frenchmen denominations of paper money below fifty francs—say ten dollars; Germany similarly treats her people; but Americans are used to the convenience of paper money down to single dollars, and this convenience certainly will never be given up, what money Englishmen, Frenchmen, Germans, Indians, or Chinamen carry in their pockets being unimportant to us, at least as an argument. No party will ever be sufficiently powerful to force Americans to carry silver instead of paper.

But if silver cannot be made to circulate, may we not use it as a base for paper money? Why should we? We have now the gold base in common with the great

European nations, and we trade mostly with them, or when trading with others, we necessarily, as a rule, agree to pay or to accept payment in London exchange—that is, we trade on the gold base. Gold has proved itself a more stable base than silver; and what can be more important to our stupendous superstructure of credit than an immovable foundation? Do we prefer to build upon quicksand? Or, in broadening the foundation of a structure, is it well to use rock for one portion of the foundation and sand for another portion? No stronger proofs of the height of civilization in this country can be offered than that we use financial contrivances so extensively, and that gold itself is not used to the extent, possibly, of even one per cent. of our volume of business, although in every transaction the buyer and the seller, when stopping to think at all, think of the gold value of the money mentioned. Is it the duty of Congress, then, to say to the people: All this is wrong; you must carry more paper and silver in your pockets; you must use checks and drafts less, and you must use silver more; you must consider the condition of our silver miners, and favor our being upon a wabbling base—part gold, part silver? Rather, is it not the duty of Congress to recognize that nearly all the business of this country is, and necessarily must be, carried on by means of some form of credit, and therefore it must be of the greatest importance to everybody to be able to feel that the firm foundation of gold-measured or gold-valued wealth is beneath it all? Congress cannot cause us to be born again, and into the Hindu, Chinese, Japanese, or even into the Mexican or South American silver-handling type; but, through the operation of laws which favor silver, so much of the kind of money which is in every way unsuited to us may be forced into the foundations of our banking and credit system, that there may be shaken or overthrown this marvellous structure, which now so well serves our vast and intricate exchange of commodities.

1896. The United States Government strained its credit, in favoring silver for fifteen years, to November, 1893, but created no silver-handling habit among the people.

CHAPTER II.

THE MOVEMENTS OF PRICES.

THE upward and downward courses of trade and prices, recurring not with regularity but with sufficient certainty to form a basis for shrewd guessing, are yet considered inexplicable, at least by one of our greatest political economists. According to Mr. David A. Wells,[1] if I draw a correct inference, everybody is cognizant of the undulatory character of trade and price movements, but nobody can account for it. The what-has-been-must-be theory is the sum of the general knowledge that buoyancy follows depression, or *vice versa*, and that a panic is apt to come after a period of over-confidence. "Neither can it be conceived how periodical changes in prices can result from any possible law of nature, unless it can be shown that such laws exist

[1] *Recent Economic Changes.*

and operate with uniformity on the human mind and on the development of the human intellect, which has not yet been done."

I feel reluctance in stating that I do not agree with Mr. Wells, but I think it important to show, if I can, that such a "law of nature" is exactly what Mr. Herbert Spencer discovered and fully explained.[1] The great philosopher pointed out the undulatory character of all motion, with numerous illustrations from the fluttering of a vessel's pennant to the course of a planet or to the rises and falls of activities in the human body. Mr. Spencer says: "Passing from external to internal changes, we meet with this backward and forward movement under many forms. In the currents of commerce it is especially conspicuous. Exchange during early times is almost wholly carried on at fairs, held at long intervals in the chief centres of population. The flux and reflux of people and commodities which each of these exhibits becomes more frequent as national develop-

[1] *First Principles*, chapter on *The Rhythm of Motion*.

ment leads to greater social activity. The more rapid rhythm of weekly markets begins to supersede the slow rhythm of fairs. And eventually the process of exchange becomes at certain places so active as to bring about daily meetings of buyers and sellers—a daily wave of accumulation and distribution of cotton, or corn,[1] or capital. If from exchange we turn to production and consumption, we see undulations, much longer indeed in their periods, but almost equally obvious. Supply and demand are never completely adapted to each other, but each of them from time to time in excess, leads presently to an excess of the other. Farmers who have one season produced wheat very abundantly, are disgusted with the consequent low price; and next season, sowing a much smaller quantity, bring to market a deficient crop, whence follows a converse effect. Consumption undergoes parallel undulations that need not be specified. The balancing of supplies between different districts, too, entails analogous oscillations. A place at which

[1] In England *corn* means wheat, rye, barley, and corn (maize).

some necessary of life is scarce becomes a place to which currents of it are set up from other places where it is relatively abundant, and these currents from all sides lead to a wave of accumulation where they meet—a glut: whence follows a recoil—a partial return of the currents. But the undulatory character of these actions is perhaps best seen in the rises and falls of prices. These, given in numerical measures which may be tabulated and reduced to diagrams, show us in the clearest manner how commercial movements are compounded of oscillations of various magnitudes. The price of consols, or the price of wheat, as thus represented, is seen to undergo vast ascents and descents whose highest and lowest points are reached only in the course of years. These largest waves of variation are broken by others extending over periods of perhaps many months. On these again come others having a week or two's duration. And were the changes marked in greater detail, we should have the smaller undulations that take place each day, and the still smaller ones which brokers telegraph from hour to hour. The whole outline would show a complication like that of a vast ocean-swell, on whose surface there rise large billows, which themselves bear waves of moderate size, covered by wavelets that are roughened by a minute ripple.

* * * * *

"Thus, then, rhythm is a necessary characteristic of all motion. Given the co-existence everywhere of antagonistic forces—a postulate which, as we have seen, is necessitated by the form of our experience—and rhythm is an inevitable corollary from the persistence of force."

The expressions which are commonly heard among traders and speculators: "The market is tired," "It can't go one way all the time," "What goes up must come down," "Look out for a reaction," "The tide must be nearly ready to turn," and hundreds of others of a similar nature are acknowledgments of the force of a fundamental law, and it is safe to say that any business-man who goes along without recognizing, consciously or unconsciously, this all-governing law is likely to come to grief. He it is who "goes clamming at high tide," who buys vacant lots at the "top of a boom," who "gets left" with a big stock when buyers become scarce and who has nothing to sell when everybody wants to buy.

Theoretically there is no difficulty whatever in accounting for the fact that prices and activities rise and fall. The undulatory character of trade movements corresponds with all known motion, and it is no more the duty of the political economist to inquire further into the why and wherefore of the phenomenon than it is his business to ask why over-exertion makes him tired, why a current makes eddies, why exaltation leads to depression, why scarcity leads to glut and low prices, and glut and low prices to scarcity and high prices, or why force and resistance have any place in nature.

Recognizing that rhythm in motion is all-prevading, although perhaps never thinking of it as rhythmical, the shrewd man of business will attempt to measure the forces and resistances which, at a given time, result in carrying prices upward or downward or in holding them nearly stationary. And much of his success must depend upon his ability to measure correctly.

But there has been a downward movement in prices which has been going on ever since the year 1872, and while the undulatory character of the movement has not been wanting, yet the result of it has been to put the average of general prices upon a very low plane, although not lower for many staples than was ever known before. Mr. Edward Atkinson points out[1] that the necessaries of life were lower in 1845–1850 than they are now, but, nevertheless, quite a revolution has taken place, and there are many individuals who attribute this fall in prices to the "outlawry" or the "demonetization" of silver, in spite of the fact that there has been neither outlawry nor demonetization properly so-called.

Criticising the subject-matter of the first chapter in this volume, when about to be

---

[1] Testimony before **House Committee** on Coinage, Weights, and Measures, 1891.

published in *Lippincott's Magazine*, Mr. John A. Grier, having, with my consent, my manuscript before him, wrote an article for the same number of *Lippincott's* in which he said: "In 1873, when the United States outlawed silver as full legal-tender money, we blindly committed an absurd national mistake that has cost the mass of our people the loss of untold millions of dollars annually.[1]

"Only a small part of this has legally, but unfairly, enriched a few thousands of our own people, while many millions have been uselessly thrust upon our creditors on the other side of the Atlantic. The late Mr. Manning, Secretary of the Treasury, in his annual report of December 6, 1886, distinctly expressed this view of the case. Mr. Manning was a believer in the efficacy and necessity of international treaties in the use of silver as full legal-tender money. Thus, in advocating such treaties he urged

---

[1] **The United States merely** stopped the coinage of silver dollars, the country using only paper from 1862 to 1879. No effect of this stoppage was noticed for a long while; people do not agree on the reasons for the stoppage; **and nobody** can prove that prices are lower *in consequence of* the stoppage.

us to discontinue the silver coinage, so as to bring a more direct financial pressure on all other nations for the gold of the world. He thought if we should abandon the coinage of silver and more earnestly enter the greedy, grasping contest for gold then going on, we should be the gainers. With our immense natural resources in the production of so many of the articles Europe must have, we could procure the gold, while we could deny ourselves of part of our imported luxuries. In regard to the cost to us of the demonetization of silver, he said : 'The monetary dislocation has already cost our farming population, who number nearly one half the population of the United States, an almost incomputable sum, a loss of millions upon millions of dollars every year, a loss which they will continue to suffer so long as Congress delays to stop the silver purchase and by that act to compel an international redress of the monetary dislocation.'

"To give some estimate of these losses I have made the following investigations. If we assume that it required, approximately, the same amount of labor to farm an acre of cereals during the three years, 1871, 1872, and 1873, that it did during the three years 1886, 1887, and 1888, then by an examination of the farm price of cereals as given by the U. S. Statistical Bureau, it will be seen that, on a gold valuation at each period, the annual shrinkage in the price received by the farmers for cereals during the latter period was about $600,000,000. It can be seen by an examination of the United States statistics that for the five years 1885–1889, as compared with the five years 1880–1884, our exportation of wheat and wheat-flour fell off in value to the enormous extent of $334,-000,000. In bushels the decrease amounted to about 159,000,000. . . . Although Mr. Manning was opposed to our continuing the silver-dollar coinage, we agree with him that the 'monetary dislocation' was one of the main causes in the loss of a part of our foreign trade and the value of our products. While this loss in the price of cereals is so great, perhaps the loss on the other products of the farm was equally large. The farmers of the United States, who have felt this financial grip so heavily for so many years, are carefully studying the question. They have apparently reached some unwise conclusions as to the proper remedies, but, if we can judge aright, they, as a class, have determined that silver shall be restored. As to the statistical facts cited above, all have ready access to our government statistics, and if you see fit you can collate them, and then the facts will depend upon the reliability of these reports. There are a few eminent statistical and financial authorities who deny that the disuse of silver as a money-measuring metal has had any effect in causing the world-wide fall in prices or on our loss of certain foreign exports! They admit the changes, but attribute them to other causes. This is one of those inductive questions that each one must settle for himself. Perhaps Mr. Cowperthwait has not the least suspicion that the disuse of silver has played any part in this world-wide depression in prices. However, the British Royal Commission, appointed a few years ago to examine exhaustively this question, unanimously admitted this important conclusion. Six of the twelve called for the prompt restoration of silver, while the other six hesitated for further observation. Thus, by the novel attempt to get down to a gold basis, which Mr. Cowperthwait calls 'an immovable foundation,' we found ourselves measuring prices by a commodity for which the legal demand had suddenly and largely increased. We also found that its value, either as a commodity or as money, has largely appreciated. There is no other way to ascertain the exchangeable value of money than to see what it will exchange for or buy in the markets of the world. Tested by this inexorable economic rule, it will be found that the average prices of commodities used in common life have fallen approximately one third since the demonetization of silver in 1873. This simply means that the purchasing power of gold has increased about one half, or fifty per cent. If the greatest possible stability in the purchasing power of coined money is desirable, then by all means let us maintain the concurrent use of both metals, in order to maintain their mutual automatic action on each other's value. To measure by silver alone would be as unwise as to measure by gold alone. We might as wisely abandon the use of two metals in the construction of the pendulum of our most perfect clocks or of the balance-wheel of our chronometers. The pendulum and balance-wheel were an evolution in practical mechanics, and, with all our scientific advances, we do not abandon this use of the two metals. There is abundant evidence on all sides that the civilized world will not abandon the use of either silver or gold as money-measuring metals. The apprehensions entertained by Mr. Cowperthwait that we, like China, India, or Mexico, may perchance reach a silver basis, are groundless, although we may decide to increase very largely our use of silver. There is a wide and safe margin between this increased use of silver and free coinage. Silver mono-metallism is repudiated even by the free-coinage advocates. The nation will hardly maintain a policy which no one wants.

"Up to 1873 the burden of measuring debts throughout the civilized world rested substantially on the two metals, gold and silver. The demonetization of silver in 1873 was an attempt to change this basis to gold alone. Then such was the enormous legal demand for gold that its value as a commodity was advanced, and hence its value as money. Prices then began to fall, as they were regulated by this appreciated gold. This is the simple explanation of the injurious part of the fall in prices. Measuring the value of wheat and cotton bought here at gold prices, which could be bought in India at silver prices, accounts for much of the loss of profit in our foreign trade in such commodities. The outlawry of silver produced a great part of this change, but not all of it. This portion we can change by national legislation. A fall in prices is not an unmixed evil, but a fall in prices when the cost of production has not been equally reduced to the producer is an evil that the producer will do his best to remove."

This sounds well, but before the Messrs.

Lippincott were able to print (October, 1891) for the November number of the magazine Mr. Grier's article and mine, the farmers of the United States were in the midst of jubilation over their enormous crops, and I fear that some callous farmers were rejoicing too over the partial failure of crops abroad. Let us hope that our farmers continued their careful study of the silver question after the financial grip had been relaxed, and that some of them used different spectacles in the fall of 1891 from the ones used in the spring of 1891. In a time of adversity silver-tongued orators, who charge all woes to "demonetization," would naturally receive more attention than they would receive in a time of prosperity, the ups and downs of life and the periods of high and of low prices affecting the farmer as the merchant and the manufacturer.

As a rule, taking years together, the farmer sells at low prices when he is compensated for this by being able to buy at low prices, or he pays largely when he receives largely. But at this writing[1] he is

[1] Winter of '91–'92.

selling great crops at *high prices* while he is still buying at *low prices* any articles that he may need.

Few farmers get rich; so do few other strivers after wealth; and it is no less important for the farmer than for anybody else to notice that improvements everywhere are revolutionizing farming, trade, commerce, transportation, and all business. Events move very fast nowadays, and he who would succeed must "keep up with the procession."

I think that the late Mr. Manning's sagacity in seeing that the government ought to stop the purchasing of silver entitles him to forgiveness for mistaking *bullion-value dislocation* for *monetary dislocation*, and to forgiveness for not seeing why the prices of commodities had declined. Indeed, until *Recent Economic Changes* appeared few people could have understood the reasons for this decline. The Royal Commission made its final report in 1888, and the members of it were not much better informed regarding the direct action of economic changes upon prices than was the late Mr.

Manning, but the commission itself did not advise England to purchase silver; and if the commission had been considering the silver question from our point of view we should not have been advised to purchase silver either. The commission was quite as sensible as Mr. Manning when it reported, as it did report, "No settlement of the difficulty is, however, in our opinion, possible without international action."[1]

In order to show how much the farmers have lost by "dislocation" or "demonetization" or "outlawry," Mr. Grier makes the violent assumption that it required in 1886, 1887, and 1888 the same amount of labor to farm an acre of cereals as it did in 1871, 1872, and 1873, and I note that Mr. Grier overlooks an important truth: a monetary change could not affect the farmer in the prices of the things which he sells differently from the way such monetary change must affect him in the prices of the things which he buys—a monetary change which makes him sell lower necessarily enabling him to buy lower. But

[1] *Silver in Europe*, p. 272, S. Dana Horton.

on the average it did not require, in 1886, 1887, and 1888, anything like so much labor to farm an acre of cereals as was required in 1871, 1872, and 1873, the intervening fifteen years being wonderfully prolific in labor-saving inventions. Small farmers could not obtain a profit in the later period as easily as in the earlier period, because much of the agricultural machinery of our time is unsuited to small farms, and because the development of vast farms has been accompanied by a fall in the prices of farm products, cheaper processes and augmented production bringing about their inevitable results. By similar means in the same period of fifteen or twenty years great businesses have swept small businesses out of existence; but however much we may dislike the results we cannot fairly charge them to any monetary change, either real or imaginary.

Imaginary indeed is the "dislocation," the "outlawry," and the "demonetization" about which, because of "damnable iteration," we have grown so tired of hearing. A great decline has taken place in the price of silver bullion, but nobody sells merchandise for silver bullion, and its price movements concern very few people. What people generally are concerned about is the prices at which they buy and sell merchandise, stocks, bonds, or any valuable thing. Intrinsically, silver coins are worth, in gold, say thirty per cent.[1] less than their face value, and we may add that paper money is intrinsically worth nearly one hundred per cent. less than its face value, but the face value itself is all that concerns you, whenever you use the paper or the silver coins in buying or selling anything. If silver coins were not receivable in settlement of debts, if you could not buy goods with them, or if you could not exchange them for gold coins, at the face value of each, then "dislocation," or "outlawry," or "demonetization" might be fairly charged, but the untruth of the charge is demonstrated thousands of times every day, on each side of the Atlantic, ten silver dollars buying as much as a golden eagle will buy, twenty shillings being as valuable as is a sovereign, twenty

[1] 1896. Fifty per cent.

francs as a napoleon, and twenty marks as a *doppelkrone*. If an act of demonetization or outlawry had been passed by the American Congress, or by the legislatures of England, France, or Germany, the equality in the purchasing power of gold and silver coins would have been overthrown. Instead of complaining of the so-called results of an imaginary demonetization of silver, we should be thankful that our legislation, in favor of silver, has not yet resulted in the demonetization of gold.

But if we deny that silver has been either demonetized or outlawed, and deny also that the fall in the price of silver bullion has caused the fall in the prices of commodities, how shall we account for the latter? Fortunately this part of the silver question has been gone over in great detail and been treated in a masterly way by Mr. Wells, in his *Recent Economic Changes*, the volume already quoted; and nobody can be better informed upon such changes than he, in spite of the appearance that in his general reading there did not happen to be included a certain chapter in Herbert Spencer's works.

A stock argument of the silver advocate is this: Because silver and commodities have declined together—cause and effect in his mind—therefore, if you advance the price of silver you will advance the prices of commodities. A careful study of the general decline in prices, however, will show that silver and commodities have felt the force of great economic changes, these changes being the cause of the downfall in almost all prices, that of silver included. Any man of business familiar with one or more articles of trade or commerce which have fallen in price, or familiar with the decline in freight and transportation rates during the period since the very high range of 1872, can see that invention and discovery have, one or the other or both, put down prices and rates at least in particular instances; and we have yet to hear of a case of decline which can be attributed to the decline in silver, excepting, of course, in goods manufactured from this metal.

Invention and discovery have played a great part in the decline of silver itself, new mines and new processes yielding greatly increased production; and if we take any of the staple articles, iron, steel, petroleum, cottons, woollens, paper, quinine, tea, coffee, sugar, beef, wheat, etc., etc., a similar story is told of a revolution accomplished or now progressing, everything being put upon the market at much lower cost than ever before. Nothing is easier than to say that prices in general have fallen, because silver has fallen: nothing can be more difficult than to prove the connection. The appearance at the same time of two or more phenomena suggests cause and effect; and so when "demonetization" is pointed out as the cause of the decline in the price of silver, and this "demonetization" and this decline are pointed out as the cause of the decline in general commodities, these statements naturally find believers, although there is no better reason for attributing the fall in general prices to the fall in the price of silver, than there would be for attributing the fall in the price of silver to the fall in general prices. Certainly no fair-minded person can read Mr. Wells' book without becoming fully convinced that the fall in the prices of commodities and the fall in the rates for transportation are directly due to the force of irresistible economic changes, silver itself being forced down with other things, anti-silver legislation as a force, in comparison, having little appreciable effect.

Not content with proving the naturalness, so to speak, of the fall in prices, Mr. Wells shows, too, that the fall is far from being such an unfortunate thing as the "silverites" claim it to be. Instances of both the naturalness of the decline in price and the benefit of that decline are afforded by a great number of articles of which, for example, quinine is notable. Formerly the medicinal preparation sold at over one dollar per ounce, and, in a time of civil war in New Granada, it advanced to over four dollars per ounce, but in those times quinine was manufactured solely from that cinchona-bark which could be obtained from trees in the forests of the northern states of South America. Now the trees are cultivated in the East Indies; these trees yield more than the indigenous trees of South America, and by " new and more economical processes more quinine can now be made at less cost in from three to five days than could have been effected by old methods in twenty days." The fall in the price of quinine is hard upon those South Americans who used to get high prices for their bark, but the benefit to multitudes of human beings cannot be questioned. We may accentuate the bearing of the experience of quinine upon the silver question by remarking that both the South Americans who have lost and the East Indians who have gained are handlers of silver money; therefore, adopting the views of the " silverites," excluding natural causes, the decline of silver has been the cause of a transfer of business from one silver-using community to another silver-using community! What the " silverites " would say regarding the benefit derived by all other communities from the cheapening of quinine, no matter what moneys they use, we can not guess.[1]

[1] N. Y. market price of quinine, 1891, about twenty cents an ounce.

1896. Quinine is about one third higher in price than in 1891, and silver is as much lower.

In the most natural manner, too, the business of tea cultivation and tea exportation seems to be in process of transfer from China to India, India having adopted important improvements. The world is benefited by obtaining tea at very low cost, although Chinamen have never raised a hand against silver, and although the people of India use silver now as they always have used it.[1]

Then the beet-sugar industry has been built up largely at the expense of the cane-sugar industry, and this without regard to the circumstance that the Europeans engaged in raising beets and in making beet-sugar have to work upon the gold basis, while some of the countries, whose people are interested in cane-sugar, are upon a silver basis, and at least one, Cuba, upon a paper basis. But the world now gets very low-priced sugar.

A single day's observation of the industries about him will yield to anybody sufficient evidence of overwhelming industrial changes, all toward a lower cost of production. A little study will show that

[1] 1896. India, while still gaining in tea cultivation, is losing confidence in silver as perfect money.

in the past quarter of a century more important results have been attained by industrial development than in fifty previous years. If anything else has forced prices downward, that other thing must have had a comparatively insignificant effect. There is left no part of the decline in prices to be so accounted for; industrial development not monetary change accounts for the whole decline; the action of industrial development is direct and is apparent to all; the monetary change, as charged, is itself denied, and if it could have caused any part of the decline in prices, its action is obscure and the measurement of the effect of the action must be left to guessing. Price movements used to be charged to currency movements but the theory was exploded long before Mr. Spencer penned the lines herein quoted, and he had no occasion to attribute price movements to changes either in the volume of money or the sum *per capita*. Due attention is given to this old currency theory in another chapter of this book.

CHAPTER III.

INDIA AND HER SILVER RUPEE.[1]

Much has been said of the advantages which India has enjoyed through the cheapening of silver, the farmer and planter of India receiving now, it is claimed, as many *rupees* for their crops as formerly, while the American farmer and planter receive fewer dollars than formerly. And the fact of the *rupee* retaining only its old purchasing power while the dollar has a higher purchasing power, is offered as evidence that instead of the supposed

---

[1] The rupee is the standard unit of **value of India and** also a silver coin of India, nominally worth forty-**eight cents or two** English **shillings.** The market value of **rupees changes hourly with** the market **value of silver** bullion. At this writing *rupees* **are worth** in London only the equivalent of **thirty-four cents** each, silver bullion being down to ninety-five cents per ounce.

1896. The present **value of the rupee is** about **twenty-four cents.**

depreciation of silver, what has occurred is an *appreciation of gold.* When arguing in this manner the "silverite" loses sight of the circumstance that silver dollars will buy in America, just as much as gold dollars will buy, and that silver coins are equal in purchasing power to gold coins in most European countries, provided you wish to buy goods in the country which has issued the coins. Whether we speak of appreciation or depreciation, the question therefore must lie between the *rupee* and *money* generally, not between the *rupee* and gold. In many parts of this book, proof is given of the truth of the theory that *prices have declined* and reasons are given for believing that *money has not appreciated.* Simply stating here, that if money had appreciated real-estate and rents and wages would have gone down, which they have not, and interest rates would have gone up, which they have not, we may well confine our present attention to India and to her silver *rupee.*

It has been pointed out that the wheat and cotton of India are sold in Liverpool in competition with American wheat and cotton, and that the Oriental, because of willingness to receive silver, while we exact gold, has an advantage of twenty or thirty per cent. over American competitors.[1] The Oriental producer and exporter have been growing rich at our expense, it is said, and the really great industrial progress which India has made in the past decade or so is triumphantly referred to as the natural result of India's holding to the silver basis.[2] Strange as it may seem, the silver advocate does not call attention to the Oriental importers and to the Oriental consumers of foreign goods. Are these people growing rich, too, or do they find that foreign goods have to be paid for with gold? And if the producer and exporter gain twenty or thirty per cent., because *exportations* are paid for in silver, must not the importer and consumer lose twenty or thirty per cent. because *importations* have to be paid for in gold? In other words, through the medium of

---

[1] 1896. Now about fifty per cent.

[2] India had made great strides in railway development, and vast new areas are now reached by trade and commerce.

foreign trade, must not some people in India be rapidly obtaining possession of the wealth of other people in India? And at a twenty-or-thirty-per-cent. rate the transfer of the total wealth of India from some pockets to others will not take very long; indeed, it ought to have been accomplished some years ago!

In truth, however, India carries on foreign trade in the manner pursued by other countries—she both buys and sells commodities on the gold basis of value, and the contrivance of *foreign exchange* is the means of purchase and sale, silver not being received in direct payment for exportations of merchandise, and gold not being sent away in direct payment for importations of merchandise, as a general thing. The producer receives money in the form of silver *rupees* from the exporter, but the exporter draws a commercial bill of exchange on London, and this bill of exchange is for gold. Conversely, the Indian importer of merchandise pays for that merchandise in gold in London, providing money or credit there to meet a bill of exchange drawn against him, although this same importer sells the merchandise in India, and for silver *rupees*. The *rupee* is suitable for the interior business of India, but when Indian products reach the seaports, and when foreign products come to these seaports, the bullion value of the *rupee* has to be taken into the calculation, and the changes in that bullion value must necessarily be reflected throughout India, whether the result be to hold such prices up as would otherwise go down, or to put such prices up as would otherwise remain stationary. The competition among Indian *importers* forces them to pay as high gold prices as possible and to sell for as low silver prices as possible. The competition among Indian *exporters* forces them to pay as high silver prices as possible and to sell for as low gold prices as possible. This double competition adjusts the prices of exportable and importable goods, in India, as elsewhere; and there, as throughout the commercial world, the competition helps to adjust, also, the prices of domestic goods when sold for domestic consumption. This fact should not be lost sight of: the unit of value of India, the *rupee*, constantly changes in price, the price moving upward and downward with the price of Mexican dollars or of other silver moneys of the Orient, all of them following closely the fluctuations in the price of silver bullion.[1] If you use the money of the United States or Canada, or of most of Europe, you can buy commodities, on the average, at prices say thirty per cent. below the average of 1872, and there are many reasons for this decline in prices. If you cannot buy at low prices, with Indian *rupees*, Mexican dollars, or Eastern silver money, still when you do change your money into these moneys you obtain, say thirty per cent. more of these moneys than you could have obtained in 1872. You can buy at low prices with good money, or you can buy at high prices with depreciated money, and not make any better bargain in either case. And you may be very sure that the great merchants of India, China, and the East generally watch closely the price of the *rupee*, the Mexican dollar, and of silver

[1] Mexican dollars circulate extensively in the East.

bullion on the London market, and regulate their own prices of commodities in accordance therewith.

The declining value of silver has given a slight advantage to Oriental producers and exporters of merchandise over Oriental importers and consumers, and the flow of silver to the East has been accelerated by the willingness of Europe to get rid of silver or, let us say, a willingness to give more silver for Oriental products than formerly. When silver declines a fraction, foreign exchange in the East is affected at once; exporters of merchandise must find it easier to transact business, and importers must find difficulty, until prices adjust themselves to the new conditions. Or, looking on silver as a commodity, we can see that for many years, because of a low price, the East has been able to obtain easily large quantities of silver. Apparently, silver being the money of the East, this accumulation of silver has been advantageous. Is the advantage real or nominal? There is now such an abundance of silver in the East as to make what has been called a state of congestion, and there is no outlet for the metal. Other countries have willingly given silver for Oriental products, but these countries will not give their own products in exchange for the same silver. The Secretary of the United States Treasury, Mr. Foster, in a letter to the banker's convention, November, 1891, speaking of the decline in the price of silver, goes on to say :

"Other causes, which I cannot enlarge upon, have operated to produce this result, prominent among which is the large falling off in the shipments of silver to India and China. The shipments of silver from London to India during the first nine months of the present calendar year show a reduction of over $17,000,000 as compared with the same period of the prior year, while the shipments of silver to China show even a greater decrease."

India and China have a plethora of that kind of money which great commercial countries do not want, and India and China seem to have discovered, just when the value of silver is very low, that they cannot take so freely of such money. Of course, if the United States should adopt free coinage of silver, then it might appear that the heathens were longer-headed than now seems evident. They could sell us silver then at a good profit over the cost. But at this moment it is too soon to contend that Oriental countries have been benefited by the decline in the value of silver. In the early years of our war, both in the North and in the South, it was not difficult to sell goods for paper money, and it was comparatively easy to accumulate paper money and paper-money obligations; but a little later the positions of the money accumulators in the two sections drifted farther and farther apart, as it became clear in the North that the paper money of the United States would appreciate, and as it became clear in the South that the paper money of the Confederacy would depreciate. So the question whether India and China and other silver-money countries have actually been benefited by the opportunity to accumulate silver must depend largely upon the future price of silver.[1]

[1] Written in 1891.

Corroborative of such a view, although doubtless not intended to be so, I think, is the testimony of Mr. F., a New York exporter, before the House Committee on Coinage, Weights, and Measures, February, 1891. Speaking of our ability to compete with Russia in the shipping of oil to the East, Mr. F. said:

"It is a matter of exchange. It is relative to the gold value of silver. It is what we call the fall or rise in exchange. All our exchanges in silver-using countries are regulated by the gold value of silver in London. The banker makes his quotations in exchange in China or India, on London, by the telegraphic price of silver on the London market on that day, and therefore the price of silver governs the exchanges of the silver-using countries all over the world. As a singular confirmation of what I say with regard to Russian oil during the last year, some of the refiners asked me about this question of exchange, why it was they were having such a demand for their oil. I explained the whole matter to them. I drew up a schedule showing the quotations of oil in sterling, and as silver rose in gold value oil rose in sterling."

From which it appears that every advance in the market price of silver helps us in exporting merchandise to silver-using countries. Doubtless every decline in the market price of silver helps us in our importing of merchandise from silver-using countries. In one case we are more ready to sell merchandise, because we receive *appreciated* money in payment. In the other case we are more ready to buy merchandise, because we are allowed to pay for it with *depreciated* money. The fact that we both buy and sell in London exchange is offset by the rate of exchange being controlled by the market price for silver bullion at the time of each transaction. It has been shown that the East more easily sells goods and more easily accumulates silver when silver is down in price than when silver is up; and, necessarily, the East more easily buys goods and has more difficulty in accumulating silver when silver is up than when silver is down.

The accumulation of silver in the East brings to mind the accumulation of silver in the United States Treasury. In so far as a decline in silver helps the exportation of merchandise from a country, that decline helps the accumulation of silver in that country; not that silver need be used in direct payment for merchandise, but because silver bullion is a commodity, and because important sums of silver coins vary in price with this commodity. Comparing to-day's market price of silver bullion with the much higher average of the past ten or fifteen years, it is fair to say that if India had frequently offset favorable trade balances by purchases of British consols or of United States bonds, and so had avoided importing so large a quantity of silver, a portion of India's loss from the depreciation of silver would have been saved; and it is fair also to say that if the United States had collected less money in the form of taxes and had accumulated a correspondingly smaller sum of silver, the government issuing or permitting to be issued other paper money than silver notes, our people would be better off than they are now. If the exportation of merchandise could be facilitated by the Treasury's buying an increased amount of silver per month, still, in the absence of any assurance that the Treasury can ever sell its silver, such buying, for such a purpose, would be foolhardy.

I am told that "Some of the large Indian native bankers have been so disturbed by the late violent fluctuations in silver that they have begun to carry part of their reserve in gold." I do not know how far this custom extends, but I should think it likely to grow.

NOTE.—The flow of silver to India is not increased by the high nominal value which is placed on silver in the coinage of *rupees*. In our mint, 16 ounces of silver are called equal to one ounce of gold; in the mints of the Latin union, 15½ to 1 is the ratio; and in coining *rupees* only 15 ounces of silver are supposed to be needed to represent the value of one ounce of gold. But no mint in the world buys silver bullion at any price above the market price, excepting those mints which use depreciated coins to pay for the bullion. It is not important to the seller of bullion to receive high prices in depreciated coins, rather than low prices in money which has not depreciated.

NOTE TO THIRD EDITION, 1896.—The Indian mints stopped coining *rupees* in June, 1893. The distress from money depreciation had become great, particularly among the wage-earning and salary-earning classes. Their incomes had not been proportionately advanced—never are in such cases. India may now be cited as a horrible example instead of an example to follow.

CHAPTER IV.

PRICES AND WAGES.

THE silver advocate may not be convinced that the cause of the fall in prices is an industrial progress hitherto unparalleled, although, if he would look in the direction of the facts, they would stare at him from every vast farm, every great factory, every fast or cheaply run steamship or railway train, and from every modernly managed industry. If he be obstinate on the subject of the cause of the decline in prices, then, what will he say to this bold statement?— the decline itself has been a good thing for the world. Evidently, whatever may be said regarding the cause of the fall in prices, it will be folly to continue to complain, provided we can show that the fall has been, on the whole, beneficial.

A fall in the price of an article is, generally speaking, a benefit to the buyers and an injury to the sellers of that article. A fall in the prices of many articles is a benefit to many buyers and an injury to many sellers. In this limited view of the case one man's loss is another man's gain, and if the number of buyers and the number of sellers were equal, the whole community could neither gain nor lose by either a rise or a fall in prices, for the quantity of things bought necessarily equals the quantity of things sold. But it is not true that there are in any community as many sellers as there are buyers; on the contrary, the buyers far outnumber the sellers, always and everywhere. Everybody is a buyer, but that great proportion of the people who (themselves and their families) have fixed incomes, who live by fees for professional services, who earn salaries, and who earn wages, are not sellers. And if a vast proportion of the population obtain money without selling anything but their time or labor, and if they pay out their money for all kinds of merchandise, then it follows that a fall in the prices of merchandise must benefit the vast majority. Now, this benefit would not be so clear if it could be shown that incomes, fees, salaries, and wages had gone down with the prices of commodities. To the best of my knowledge, however, while incomes from investments have declined and rich people have had to be content with smaller incomes, yet there is no proof that fees, salaries, and wages have declined at all. *There is proof, indeed, that wages have advanced.* Wage-earners and their families alone make up a majority of the people, and if wage-earners now receive more money than formerly, while everything the wage-earner buys can be bought for less money than formerly, how shall we escape from the conclusion that the wage-earners have been benefited by the decline in the prices of commodities? And if the majority have been benefited, then how can it be contended that the fall in prices has been a bad thing? Certainly many individuals and many communities have been hurt when other individuals and other communities have captured the former's industries, but the law of the survival of the fittest holds absolute sway, and it is worse than useless to quarrel with it. We may offer sympathy to the unfortunate ones, but cannot help thinking that their misfortune is due to their inability to keep up with the lightning speed of the time. The world has not stepped backward, and the times cannot be far out of joint, when employers of laborers can afford to pay more for labor than ever before. The employers of to-day do better for the community than the employers of yesterday, both in selling goods at lower prices and in paying out more money to each of their employees, and while we should not undervalue the sympathy which is due to those employers who have been beaten, yet we ought not to withhold congratulation from those employers who have succeeded. They, and the inventors and discoverers allied with them, have given the world its necessary articles and its luxuries at lower prices than ever before, and without reducing the sum annually paid to the workmen employed.

The vital point in the silver question lies in the rate of earnings of laborers and of all workmen, and it is strange that the House Committee on Coinage, Weights, and Measures, when reporting on the Senate Silver Bill,[1] should have touched so lightly upon this wage question. Even if we admit, for the sake of argument, what is plainly absurd, that prices have fallen because of "demonetization," yet if the fall in prices has not been accompanied by a fall in wages to at least so great an extent, then the fall in prices must in itself be accounted a good thing. That is to say, "demonetization," from the "silverite's" point of view, has been the means of enabling wage-earners to either live better or to save more than they could when they had to pay higher prices for everything—a majority of the community are better off than they used to be. And if wage-earners are well off, then also must be well off a large portion of the minority, for money paid in wages is at once returned through retail trade.

However, the majority of the committee reporting against free coinage say nothing in their report about wages, while the mi-

[1] 1891.

nority, in favor of free coinage, content themselves with an if or two, and with some unwarranted assumptions, one of which is that labor organizations have been able to keep up the rates of wages for the past seventeen or eighteen years, and another that the number of unemployed persons is sufficiently large to offset the rate, it being, of course, true, as the minority say, that "the effect of an appreciating standard of value can never be determined by considering merely the quantity of commodities which the laboring man *who happens to have work* can buy with his dollar *when he gets it*." Now, we may differ in opinion as to the power of labor organizations, but this point is not important, for no matter how the rate of wages has been maintained, *if the rate has been maintained*, then wage-earners have been benefited by the fall in prices. The question of the power of labor organizations does not enter into the subject. If wages have not fallen during the past seventeen or eighteen years, while prices of everything which the wage-earner buys have fallen, then the wage-earner's gain is proved beyond question. Those who think that workmen have held up wages through the power of organization, may agree with others that the fact of wage-rates being high, while prices are low, is evidence that wage-earners have no right to complain of "demonetization." So far as I know, the "silverites" have not yet claimed that labor could have been organized more effectively but for "demonetization"!

Without offering any proof, the minority of the committee assert: "We do know that during the last seventeen or eighteen years an unusually large number of men have been out of employment, both in Europe and America, and that the cry of hard times has been heard almost continuously throughout the whole civilized world." And the minority say too: "It will be admitted by everybody that the laboring classes, as a whole, cannot be permanently prosperous in the face of general business depression. It will also be admitted, we presume, that the period extending from 1873 down to the present time, has been one of very unusual depression all over the commercial world." I fear that the minority took advantage of the feeling of depression which actually existed at the time the report was made. This period extended from November, 1890, the date of the panic, to the fall of 1891, when our great crops were assured. If the minority were to use their language now, some people would be ready to say: "No. Times have been both bad and good since 1873; they were quite good from 1877 to the date of the shooting of Garfield in 1881, and to the occurrence of general drouth in that year, and were so good in 1879, that 'the boom of '79' was long talked about; 1886, 1887, 1889, and 1890 up to November were fairly good years, or not below the average; and then in the fall of '91 plenty of people made lots of money." The minority should have proved their assertion, and probably would have done so, if possible, by showing that pauperism had increased, or that savings-bank deposits had decreased, for such evidence is necessary to bear out the bald statement that the number of the unemployed has been unusually large.

In another place the minority contradict themselves: "We may concede that since 1873 there has been a large increase in the production of the great staples of commerce; but whatever the increase may have been the commodities have all been consumed. There is no accumulated surplus of wheat, or cotton or any other leading staple." What! Depression with a large increase in production and no accumulation? Who consumed the increased product? Necessarily the working population. And how could the workmen have obtained the money to pay for the increased product except by being well employed? The minority should have compared the statistics of the seventeen or eighteen years with the statistics of some other period of seventeen or eighteen years, or rather the minority should have compared the dozen years following January 1, 1879, the date of specie resumption, with another period of a dozen years, for between 1873 and 1879 the cheapening of silver caused silver coins to circulate, to some extent, alongside of our paper money, and up to 1879, therefore, the declining price of silver operated to augment our total circulation. The panics of '37, '57, and '73 are wholly unconnected with the silver question, and so are the years of depression which naturally followed each of these panics, excepting that amelioration may have come from cheap silver after 1873. Were not '37, and '57 and '73 as severe as anything since experienced? Since the time when "demonetization" was first noticed (years after 1873), what years have been *unprecedentedly* prolific of disaster?

The minority have lengthened the string of unsupported assertions which make a basis for the silver theory: "Demonetization" caused the decline in silver; the decline in all prices necessarily followed; the fall in prices has been accompanied by business depression; business depression keeps an unusually large number of men out of employment, although, strange to say, those who do find it are paid good rates; and a large increase in the product of the staple articles has, somehow or other, been consumed without anybody's being able to see how in the world the consumers have been able to pay for this product. The truth is, that since 1872 the population of the world has been better fed, better clothed, and better sheltered than in any previous time. One of this same minority has lately been showing how particularly well off now are the miners in a community with which he is familiar. I take this illustration, because the "silverites" cannot question the authority, and because the illustration shows in a most admirable manner that the price of a product may decline thirty per cent. *without affecting the prosperity of the workmen engaged in producing the article.* If the decline in the market price of silver has not worked harm to silver miners, how can this decline have worked harm to laborers in any industry? Here is the charming picture of a happy community, drawn by the Hon. Horace F. Bartine of Nevada, the famous silver advocate. I quote from his letter to the *Engineering and Mining* Journal, issue of October 24, 1891:

"Every miner in the employ of John P. Jones, or any other mine owner, either in Virginia City or Gold Hill, is paid $4 a day for eight hours' work. Men working above ground receive from $3.50 to $4. There is no departure from these rates.

"With one day's wages the miner can buy 100 lbs. of the best flour in the world; or 7 bushels of the finest potatoes ever grown; or 32 lbs. of choice beef; or 32 lbs. of prime butter, and almost everything else in proportion. With the product of a month's labor he can pay his board at a first-class restaurant and have $94 left.

"I ask you in all candor how that compares with the condition of the miner or the factory hand in New York or Pennsylvania, where the employers generally express so much horror and indignation at the thought of the laboring man being paid in '80-cent dollars'?

"The Comstock miner thinks nothing of spending $50 for a day's amusement at a picnic. This may not be suggestive of rigid economy, but it certainly does not show that he is being shamefully wronged by his employer. There are, no doubt, some poor people there—sickness and misfortune invade every community.

"Attracted by the high wage-rate, more men go there than can find employment; but that is not the fault of the mine owners. They employ as many as they need, and those who obtain work are the best paid, best fed, best clothed, and most thoroughly independent class of workingmen to be found on the American continent, or on the surface of the globe."

And yet, Mr. Bartine, you and your friends would change all this! The low prices (excepting for picnics), which enable workmen to obtain all they need for less money than they can easily earn, you would change to high prices, so that, for instance, the miner shall be unable to save the "$94," or be unable ever to go on picnics at all. And Mr. Jones and other mine owners, whose business is so prosperous that they can afford to pay $3.50 to $4 for eight hours' work, want the United States to pay thirty per cent. more for silver than any other government will give for it, so that the prosperity of Mr. Jones and other mine owners shall be further enhanced! Yes, Mr. Bartine and Mr. Jones, silver-mine owners do pay better wages than other employers can afford to pay; but don't you think that mine owners and their miners already have a fair share of the country's good things? What ground have you for asking the government to continue piling up silver in its vaults at the expense of the whole tax-paying public?[1] And, Mr. Bartine, were you thinking of a section of the country with which you are less familiar, when, eight months before you wrote the lines above quoted, you helped to make out the minority report and agreed to these words?—

"Any argument based upon the assumed fact that the present condition is favorable to the wage-worker, because he can buy more commodities with his daily wage, is utterly fallacious, and fails to reach the heart of the question." It is true you follow with the irrelevant remark about labor

[1] The Silver Purchase Law was then in force.

organizations; but have you drawn a correct picture of the prosperity of Virginia City and Gold Hill, or is it merely an "assumed fact that the present condition is favorable to the wage-worker"? Can wage-workers there obtain such a quantity of the necessaries of life "with one day's wages," or can they not? Can a miner save "$94" in a month, or is this "utterly fallacious"? Or will Mr. Bartine and his friends produce a new picture of real prosperity, according to their own ideas; not a picture of what is commonly known as prosperity—say, high wages, low cost of living, and all that—but something unique and suitable to the silver question?

Corroborative of Mr. Bartine's ideas, when he was writing about the miners, is the following portion of an editorial in the *Engineering and Mining Journal* of October 10, 1891:

"From all indications the production of silver in this country will be considerably greater this year than in 1890. Never before has there been so much activity in all the silver-mining camps of the West as at present, and this is beginning to show in the greater output of ore. The lead-smelters of Denver and Pueblo are pressed to the limit of their capacity to reduce the ore of this class which is offered, and there has even been some talk of the erection of new works at the latter place. The production of lead ore has not, apparently, increased, but the smelters are running their furnaces on low lead charges, and are thus handling the greater volume of dry ores.

"The general prosperity in the silver-mining industry throughout the West is particularly noticeable, in view of the general business depression which has made itself felt throughout the past year in almost all branches of industry in the East."

It appears from this that the mining industry was in so good a position that the panic of 1890 had little or no effect upon it. That panic affected many other industries, but it is too early yet to tell whether the injury has been wholly overcome by the great crops of 1891. I do not know, however, that among the injured industries there has been any important reduction in the average rate of wages, or that there has been anywhere an important increase in the number of unemployed workmen. The silver-mining industry is in an exceptionally good position, but if industries generally had been suffering from "seventeen or eighteen years" of depression, as "silverites" charge, then these industries would have had no strength left to withstand the panic of 1890, our daily papers would have been filled with accounts of wholesale reductions in wages, and wholesale discharges of workmen, and accounts of numerous failures everywhere. From whatever cause, or in spite of any cause, the industries of this country are certainly in a fairly sound condition. The decline in prices is the only evidence that we have had "seventeen or eighteen years" of depression, but the decline has been caused by natural industrial development, and the decline in prices has been accompanied by an enormous increase in consumption, an increase impossible whenever there is real depression. During these years of so-called depression the wage-earner generally has been well employed, as proved by his ability to purchase and consume, and to-day he appears to be best employed in what should be our most depressed industry, the silver industry itself.

1896. **The general depression of 1893 and later years** was severely felt in the **silver mining industry.** Of course that industry was unfavorably affected, **Nov., 1893, by the** stopping of silver purchasing **on the** part of the **United States, and by** the stopping of silver coinage **by the** mints of India, **June, 1893.**

NOTE TO FIFTH EDITION.—The panic of 1893, **and the trade depression following it, are treated in the concluding chapter. It is now** claimed **that the** success of the free-coinage party **at the polls, in** 1896, would cause prices to **advance** at once; but **as such success would** cause financial disturbance and industrial depression, **and** therefore would take away from many workmen their opportunities to earn money, it seems clear **that the** first result **of** success must **be a** decline in both prices **and** wages. **The prospect** of actual free-coinage **would put a premium on gold, and there** would soon be a corresponding difference **between gold prices and** silver or legal tender prices, similar **to the difference** between gold prices and paper **prices from** 1862 to 1879; **but whether** legal-tender prices, on the **average,** would reach a higher level than the present level, say within **a year or so after the** election, is problematical. The actual passage **of a free-coinage law** would be doubtful, or at least far off, and the **gold premium would** fluctuate, as the chances seemed good or bad. **The** unquestionable **effect of** the success of the Silver Party at the **polls** is a reduction in the average **rate** of wages incident to industrial depression.

CHAPTER V.

PRICES, WAGES, AND LABOR-SAVING MACHINERY.

Keeping our attention upon the silver industry a moment longer, let us see how it is that the price of silver could have gone down without the decline's putting down the wages of silver miners. Mr. William H. Beck, a gentleman connected with the mining interests of Montana, testified before the committee as follows:

"In my observation in the far West, I see causes there that I think are tending very much to depreciate the value of silver. When I went to Montana, in 1886, it cost us to transport our ores from Dillon to Omaha $24 per ton. That transportation now costs $10 a ton. It cost us then to treat the ores $17 a ton. Now it costs $8 and $10. Mining powder cost us 50 and 60 cents a pound. We can buy it now for

20 and 22 cents a pound. It cost us then to board a man $1 a day and more. We can do it now for a less sum. Machinery is better, and improvements in mining machinery are being continually made. Concentration of ores is extending very largely. Many of our ores that were considered of no value a few years ago are now quite profitable.

"When I first went to Colorado, in 1878, the superintendent of a silver mill at Georgetown told me that he could not afford to treat ores that assayed less than $20 to the ton. By concentration, ores can now be profitably handled that yield as low as $5 a ton. By using scientific processes of treatment, low-grade ores, running 2 or 3 ounces of silver and 3 or 4 or 5 per cent. in lead, will yield a good profit. In 1889 I went to Patricroft, about 15 miles from Manchester, England, and spoke with the owner of a large smelter located at that place. He showed me a lot of ores, and finally some slag, which he stated worried him, as he would have to melt it over again. He said that it carried 1 ounce of silver to the ton. I said, 'Can you derive any profit from melting that down for 1 ounce of silver?' and he said, 'Yes, there is a small profit.' What an immense field there is when you can handle cheaply low-grade ores."

It should be noticed that Mr. Beck says nothing about any reduction in the rate of wages paid to silver miners. Apparently there has been no reduction, and certainly, there was no necessity for a reduction in wages. The decline in the cost of mining silver is accounted for in the same way that we have to account for the decline in the cost of producing other articles—general improvement in processes. The lower cost means neither lower profits nor lower wages, nor is there in the lower cost any evidence of hard times. If the minority of the committee could have shown that silver-mining has become unprofitable, that wages have been reduced, or that miners are unable to find employment, the minority would have done so. In the absence of further evidence it is fair to say that the silver-mining industry itself denies the statement that we have passed through "seventeen or eighteen years" of business depression.

Hon. Joseph H. Walker, of Massachusetts, a member of the majority of the committee, in cross-examining Mr. Francis G. Newlands, of Nevada, said:

"I hand you this table of prices, in bushels of grain, as an answer to your assertion that the farmers are suffering from a depression of prices. This shows that their products, bushel for bushel, will buy more than ever before":

Prices agreed upon by Messrs. **Kingsland & Douglas,** *successors of Kingsland, Fergeson, & Co., Simmons Hardware Company, and Mansur & Tibbetts Implement Company, all of St. Louis, Mo.*

Implements.	Money in—		1889, in bushels of—			1873, in bushels of—		
	1889.	1873.	Wheat.	Corn.	Oats.	Wheat.	Corn.	Oats.
One-horse steel plow (wood beam)	$2.75	$6.50	3.8	8.5	11.5	6.4	19.1	27.0
Two-horse steel plow (wood beam)	12.00	20.00	16.4	37.5	50.0	19.6	58.8	83.3
One-horse iron plow (wood beam)	2.00	5.00	2.7	6.2	8.3	4.9	14.7	20.8
Two-horse iron plow (wood beam)	8.00	13.00	10.9	25.0	33.3	12.7	38.2	54.1
Two-horse side hill or reversible plow	10.00	18.00	13.7	31.2	41.7	17.6	52.9	75.0
One potato digger	7.50	20.00	10.2	23.4	31.2	19.6	58.8	83.3
Old-fashioned tooth harrow	6.50	15.00	8.9	20.3	27.0	14.7	44.1	62.5
One-horse cultivator	3.50	7.00	4.7	10.9	14.5	6.8	20.5	29.1
Two-horse corn cultivator	15.00	28.00	20.5	46.8	62.5	27.4	82.4	116.6

Implements.	Money in—		1889, in bushels of—			1873, in bushels of—		
	1889.	1873.	Wheat.	Corn.	Oats.	Wheat.	Corn.	Oats.
One-horse mowing machine	45.00	85.00	61.6	140.6	187.5	83.3	250.0	354.1
Two-horse mowing machine	50.00	90.00	68.5	156.2	208.3	88.2	264.7	375.0
Horse rake (sulky)	20.00	30.00	27.4	62.5	83.3	29.4	88.2	125.0
Common Hunt rake (horse)	3.50	6.50	4.8	10.9	14.5	6.3	19.1	27.0
Common iron garden rake (10-tooth steel) (dozen)	3.75	12.00	5.1	11.7	15.6	11.7	35.2	50.0
One-horse horse-power	25.00	45.00	34.2	78.1	104.1	44.1	132.3	187.5
Two-horse horse-power	35.00	65.00	(*)	(*)	(*)	(*)	(*)	(*)
Reaper	75.00	95.00	(*)	—	(*)	(*)	(*)	(*)
Binder	135.00	—	184.9	421.8	562.5	[1]277.7	[1]769.2	[1]857.1
Cornsheller (one hole)	6.00	11.50	8.2	18.7	25.0	11.2	33.8	47.9
Fanning mill	15.00	25.00	20.5	46.8	62.5	24.5	73.5	104.1
Common hose (cast steel socket), per dozen	3.50	6.50	4.7	10.9	14.5	6.3	19.1	27.0
Common rakes (wood), per dozen	2.00	3.00	2.4	6.2	8.3	2.9	8.8	12.5
Scythes (Ames's grass), per dozen	7.50	16.00	10.2	23.4	31.2	15.7	47.0	66.6
Scythes (Ames's grass), per dozen	9.50	21.00	(*)	(*)	(*)	(*)	(*)	(*)
Scythe snaths (patent), per dozen	4.50	11.00	6.1	14.0	18.7	10.8	32.3	45.8
Shovel (Ames), per dozen	9.50	18.00	13.0	29.6	39.5	17.6	52.9	75.0
Spades (Ames), per dozen	10.00	18.50	13.7	31.2	41.6	18.1	54.4	27.0
Crowbars (steel)	.06	—	(*)	(*)	(*)	(*)	(*)	(*)
Crowbars (iron)	.05	.10	.06	.15	.2	.09	.29	.46

It will be observed that there is not in these figures any ground for asserting that farmers cannot afford to pay as much money to their workmen as in 1873.

The following tables also were submitted by Mr. Walker:

[1] For 1880.

Labor-Saving Machinery.

Wages in 1860 and in 1885 in dollars and in weight of gold and in grains.

Workmen.	Wages in dollars. 1860.	Wages in dollars. 1885.	Wages in grains of gold. 1860.	Wages in grains of gold. 1885.	Grains of gold percentage of increase
Factory hands:					
Dyers	$0.62	$1.00	16.0	25.7	61
Giggers	.62	.82	16.0	21.1	32
Shearers	.69	1.00	17.8	25.8	45
Plain weavers	.65	.85	16.7	21.8	31
Spinners	1.10	1.26	28.3	32.5	15
Miscellaneous:					
Leather factory beam and yard hands	1.10	1.67	31.0	43.0	39
Leather factory whiteners and skivers	1.83	2.75	47.2	70.8	50
Common laborers	1.00	1.50	25.8	38.7	50
Blacksmiths	1.50	2.00	38.7	51.6	33
Blacksmiths' strikers	1.00	1.50	25.8	27.0	50
Carpenters	1.67	2.00	43.0	51.6	20
Machinists	1.75	2.25	45.1	57.7	28
Locomotive engineers	2.40	3.20	62.0	82.4	33
Locomotive firemen	1.20	1.75	31.0	45.2	46
Average percentage of increase in weight of gold					38

Wages in 1860 and 1885 in current money and in grains of fine silver.

Workmen.	Wages in 1860.	Wages in 1885.	Wages in grains of fine silver in— 1860.	Wages in grains of fine silver in— 1885.	Percentage of increase of wages in grains of fine silver since 1860
Dyers	$0.62	$1.00	255.7	515.6	101.6
Giggers	.62	.82	255.7	422.8	65.3
Shearers	.69	1.00	284.6	515.6	82.0
Plain weavers	.65	.85	268.1	438.2	63.4
Spinners	1.10	1.26	453.7	649.6	43.1
Leather factory beam and yard hands	1.20	1.67	495.0	861.1	74.9
Leather factory, whiteners and skivers	1.83	2.75	754.9	1,418.2	87.8
Common laborers	1.00	1.50	412.5	772.4	87.4
Blacksmiths	1.50	2.00	618.7	1,031.2	66.6
Blacksmiths' strikers	1.00	1.50	412.5	773.4	87.4
Carpenters	1.67	2.00	688.9	1,031.2	52.5
Machinists	1.75	2.25	721.9	1,160.0	70.3
Locomotive engineers	2.40	3.20	990.0	1,650.0	66.6
Locomotive firemen	1.20	1.75	495.0	902.4	82.3

Average increase of wages received in ounces of fine silver over ounces received in 1860 is 63 per cent.

It should be remembered that general business was not more active in 1885 than in 1860, allowing for the fact that the industries of the country were upon a far more advanced plane in 1885 than in 1860.

Mr. Edward Atkinson, of Boston, the eminent writer and statistician, testified: "Prices have gone down, it is true; but if they had not, consumers would not have shared the benefit of the vast improvements and inventions which have been applied in the last twenty-five years— greater during the last twenty-five years, especially in the processes of agriculture, than ever before. The wage of labor is now higher than at the highest period of inflation in 1865, and the workman can buy a great deal more food, fuel, clothing, and shelter for each dollar." I take pleasure in recommending, here, to the reader who is interested in the phenomenon —*decline in prices, advance in wages*,—Mr. Atkinson's *The Industrial Progress of the Nation*. In the chapter, *Progress from Poverty*, Mr. Atkinson backs up with statistics this remark:

"It may be apparent from the data that I have submitted, that this period of steady reduction in prices since the end of the Civil War has been in fact a period of the greatest progress in material welfare ever witnessed in this or in any other country. The temporary difficulties, local distress, and congestion of labor, limited mainly to some of our great cities, have been mere incidents in the adjustment of society to new conditions of an assured abundance, such as were never before achieved. It has happened that there has been temporary want in the midst of general plenty and welfare; but this want has been limited to a very few conspicuous points, where it has perhaps attracted more attention than its proportion called for."

I might continue to offer authorities and evidence concerning the advance in wages and the decline in prices which have marked the past quarter of a century. I do not think, however, that further argument on the question of fact can be needed. It may be asked, though: If prices have been put down by the use, largely, of labor-saving machines, how is it that the rates of labor have not gone down; how is it that a machine which enables the employer to accomplish as much with ten men, for instance, as he formerly could with twenty men, does not necessarily cause ten men to be thrown out of employment, and so help to reduce the average rate of wages?

The assumption that a machine which saves labor necessarily throws laborers out of employment has been the cause of the destruction of machines by mob-violence, at different times, in most parts of the world, the extent of destruction being in proportion to the prevalence of ignorance. It is an unquestionable fact, however, that the average rate of wages is highest to-day in those countries which most generally use labor-saving machines. Of course a high wage-rate stimulates the invention of labor-saving machinery, but as a matter of fact, not mere theory, labor-saving machinery does not reduce wage-rates. Let us look more closely into this subject, first considering the value of a man's time when using a machine, compared to the value when not using a machine. The difference will show that an employer who has machinery *can afford* to pay more money to *each one* of his workmen than an employer who has not the machinery can afford to pay, other things being equal.

In 1888 I had an opportunity to observe the harvesting of grain in many parts of France and Germany, and I am sure that next to picturesqueness the most striking feature of the long lines of blue-bloused peasants working with scythes and sickles is the enormous waste of time or labor. What a hundred men and women were accomplishing in a day could have been accomplished by about ten men, assisted by mowing and reaping machines. Actually, in America, ten men were harvesting as much grain in a day as one hundred men and women were harvesting in France or Germany. Or to put the case more in exact accord with the facts, the harvesting of the grain on one thousand acres of land in our far West requires no greater number of hands than the harvesting of the grain on one hundred acres of land in France or Germany. Making due allowance for the cost of machinery, there can be no question that the American farmer can afford to pay more money to each one of his workmen than the foreigner can afford to pay to each one of his workmen. These differently situated farmers obtain similar sums of money for their crops per acre, and each farmer can afford to pay out from his receipts a similar portion for labor, but in one case that portion, less the cost of using machinery, is divided among ten persons, while in the other case that portion must be divided among one hundred persons.[1] The invention and use of agricultural machinery, then, enables farmers in America to pay high rates to individual workmen because more work can be done in a given time with machines than without them. In other words a labor-saving machine multiplies the value of the individual laborer. And the fact that a farmer

[1] The proportion of ten to one hundred is not supposed to be perfectly accurate, the intention being to show merely that a few Americans do as much work, in a given time, as is done by many Frenchmen or Germans.

can afford to pay high wage-rates (compared with European rates) makes it necessary that he shall actually pay high rates, for the value of a man's labor is not wholly unknown to himself, and the farm-owning class is being continually recruited from the farm-laboring class. There is competition among farmers for laborers, and there is a desire on the part of the laborers to better their condition. An upward step is more easily taken here than abroad, and to keep laborers in the laboring class the American farmer must offer inducements. The upward step is not so easily taken where the laborer must step into the ownership of a very large farm, instead of into the ownership of a small farm. But large farms need many men who have both judgment and muscle, and the most capable become farm-owners. Certainly the extensive use of agricultural machinery enables American farmers to pay—and forces them to pay—higher wages than European farmers are able to pay, or are obliged to pay. The words *can* and *must* are nearly interchangeable in this regard.

In Italy, I saw people treading on the grapes in order to press out the juice. Could you pay as much money to each one of twenty men, employed in this way, as you could pay to each of two or three men using a modern press?

In the factories everywhere on the Continent you see a similar lack of facilities for obtaining good results from the use of labor; and everywhere labor is poorly paid, because the results do not enable employers to pay high rates. You cannot pay money for wages except you receive money from the sale of your product, and you can receive money from the sale of your product only, as a rule, in competition with other producers. You can use for labor as much of your receipts as your competitors can use, but they can afford to pay to each workman more than you can pay to each workman, if their workmen accomplish more, individually, than your workmen accomplish.

We must not jump to the conclusion that the rate of wages should be, for instance, five times as high in the place where ten men work as in the place where fifty men work, 'to accomplish similar results. A portion of the difference goes to capital, in the way of higher interest; a portion goes for higher rent, a portion for higher profits, a portion for higher salaries, and a portion may go to the inventor of a machine. Then the apparent difference is partly wiped out by a reduction in the price of the product, but the workman can and does obtain a fair share of the benefit derived from using labor-saving machinery.

Let me try to illustrate. A labor-saving machine—one which promises to enable ten men to do what fifty men are in the habit of doing—is brought to the attention of the proprietors of a large manufactory. Careful investigation leads to the purchase, the managers of the works being fully convinced that this particular machine will prove valuable, although somewhat similar machines have proved "expensive luxuries." Entering the building, later, we find the machine set up, and the inventor or his agent making it go, but with the assistance of a bright employee who has been selected to have charge of the machine. To suppose that this bright employee has no visions of an advance in his own wages following success in his advanced position, is to suppose that he is not a bright employee. Indeed, the proprietors or the superintendent may promise an advance in wages, thus hoping to obtain the best of care and attention, and to reduce the risk of loss, natural in the operation of a new machine. Even the nine men who have been chosen to help the one first selected will expect to be paid a higher rate of wages than when doing less important work.

The machine proves to be as good as promised. Ten men now do as much as fifty men could do before the machine was introduced; and the managers of this factory will see the wisdom of paying these men a higher rate of wages, for if the rate be not advanced, a competing factory, just introducing the machine, will pay the necessary rate in order to obtain the services of men who know how to use the machine.

The value of the men's time has been enhanced, and this is known both to employers and to employees. But if ten men are now to do as much as fifty men did, what becomes of the forty men who were discharged? Well, the assumption that they were discharged is merely an assumption based, perhaps, upon another assumption that this manufactory is to produce a certain quantity of goods *and no more*. On the contrary, however, a few additional men may be employed.

The new position of this manufactory, in the struggle with competing manufactories, cannot be described as one where less money is given to individual workmen or to the whole working force: the position attained by progressive management means more money to workmen, but still greater results from the expenditure, these overbalancing the enhanced wage-rate; the new position means the ability to put more goods on the market, and at a reduced cost; and generally, it means a reduction in the selling price of the goods, in order to broaden the market for them. I think this a fair illustration of the way labor-saving machines augment production and necessitate reductions in prices, in order to make possible the sale of the increased product, and both of these without causing wages to be lowered. Reductions in the force of help in a factory because of the introduction of a labor-saving machine are not unknown, but I believe such cases are exceptional.

Reductions in the force of help in a factory because *competing factories* have introduced labor-saving machinery are more common; and; in the factories which are forced into a secondary place, there may be both a reduction in the number of hands and a reduction in the rate of wages, but an important distinction should be noticed. The progressive factory has taken steps which lead toward the absorption of the non-progressive factory's business, and in time the progressive factory, assisted by other labor-saving machines, may reach the point where it will employ most of the skilful workmen in its line, pay higher wages than other factories, turn out more goods, turn out goods of better quality, and be able to sell goods at a profit while other factories are getting no profit or, perhaps, are making a loss.

Both in farming and in manufacturing success is achieved by the use of high-priced laborers, such as are able to work with machinery, and in this way the market prices of almost everything are reduced. Scarcely ever does an employer reduce his wage-rate in order to lower the prices of his product. That would be working backward. If obliged by competition to reduce his wage-rate it would be as a last resort, for he knows that dissatisfaction among his men may result in cutting down his product of goods and in losing his best men. If beaten by competitors, he must adopt their ways, or find out still better ways for himself. He may increase his product, and by so doing make just as much money, but with a lower percentage of profit; he may buy materials to better advantage; he may stop waste; he may be satisfied with a lower rate of dividend or interest or profit; he may twist and turn about in every conceivable way to put himself on the level of his competitors, but, generally speaking, if he reduce his wage-rate or the number of his workmen he will jump from the frying-pan into the fire. The natural road to low cost, and, therefore, the ability to sell at low prices, is through machinery and high wages. In some countries the traditional penny a day is still the rate of wages, and in those countries, doubtless, this little sum may be as much as employers can afford to pay, for employers who have the benefit of this nominally cheap labor are not beating employers elsewhere, except as helped by climatic peculiarities. The rate of wages *per day* is of no importance to employers; the rate of wages, or the sum paid in wages, *in proportion to results*, is all-important.

But even if successful employers do pay high wages, still, do not labor-saving machines take the place of some laborers, considering the country as a whole? A small number of men accomplish as much as formerly was accomplished by a large number. Where are these now useless men? Again we have an assumption to deal with. Instead of a small number of men now doing what a large number used to do, a larger number of men are doing much more than the increase in number would indicate. The cheapening of goods by the use of machinery has brought more and more goods, in greater variety, within the reach of a constantly growing number of buyers, extending over vast territories, and continually advancing in power to buy and in desire to consume. Who now is satisfied with only so much as satisfied his father? Who cannot see that the luxuries of yesterday are the necessities of to-day? Progress means an ever increasing demand for new goods and more goods and an ever increasing ability to obtain them.

And no class in the community is so sure to be benefited by a progressive industrial movement as is the wage-earning class, for not only is it natural that prices should go down, but it is natural that wages should go up. And this is merely showing that the theory of progress agrees with the facts as we know them. How absurd, then, it is to charge that "demonetization" has put prices down, and what folly it is to talk of the community's having been injured by adverse silver legislation!

CHAPTER VI.

"THE DEBTOR CLASS."

ALL popular movements for cheap money or to make money more plentiful are strengthened by a good-natured desire to help along the debtors,—and it is commonly supposed that a large proportion of the community belong to this class. Therefore, if it were made clear to the people that debtors, properly so-called, are not comparatively numerous, and also that a process of money-cheapening would not be likely to help them, we should have little cause to fear the enacting of bad financial measures. These would be too unpopular to obtain the sanction of law.

The greater number of people in this country, as in every country, are wage- or salary-earners, and all of them are *creditors*, for the simple reason that they are not paid in advance. You give your time and labor to your employer, and only after the debt to you has accrued for a specified time are you paid off. Your interest lies in receiving the more valuable kind of money, where two kinds circulate. If you have been thrifty and have a credit at the savings-bank, this sum too you want payable in the better money; you cannot be benefited by a law which would compel savings-banks to receive depreciated money in settlement of mortgages, and therefore necessarily permit the payment of depreciated money, by savings-banks, to you. If you have no money saved up, but are in the habit of living from hand to mouth, still it cannot help you to receive your wages in inferior money just for the purpose of handing over this kind to the butcher and the grocer. Indeed, may not the talk of cheap money lead these men into trying to charge you more for the necessaries of life, even if a financial disturbance should prevent the wholesale butchers and grocers from advancing their prices? If prices should advance because of free coinage, as "silverites" expect, most assuredly wages will be a long way behind in the upward movement. The crisis in financial affairs would have the effect of injuring the industries of the nation; and at the same moment of time you might possibly witness an attempt to advance the average of prices, particularly retail prices, and an attempt to reduce the average rate of wages. Of course there would come about an approximate adjustment of the relation between prices and wages, but if prices should go up they would move much faster than wages would move. Prices could go up a little without any accompanying or following advance in wages. Most certainly, therefore, clerks and laborers cannot be classed with those debtors who are supposed to be in need of cheaper money, and if we leave wage- or salary-earners and their families out of account, we are compelled to search among the *minority* of the population for the future beneficiaries of cheap money.

Of course the greatest borrowers, and therefore the greatest debtors, are the national, state, and municipal governments, but we need waste no time on them, for nobody wants them to pay debts in silver and to collect taxes in gold.

And sympathy is not asked for the banking, railway, and industrial corporations which stagger under millions and millions of debt, the managing financiers having made no sign that relief is sought in cheaper money. On the contrary, these officers dread as their most dangerous foes any disturbers of confidence in the stability of the general financial situation.

Many merchants are chronic borrowers, but the smallest possible percentage of them are insolvent. Nearly all have in merchandise and in credits a sum larger than the total of their debts. There can be no advantage in selling the stock on hand for silver only instead of for good money, nor in collecting the outstanding claims in the inferior metal. Particularly sensitive also are debtor merchants to monetary derangements.

Some farmers and planters, however, have been loud in their demands for unlimited coinage of silver. Possibly it is thought that the difficulties which from time immemorial have beset the paying of interest on mortgages and the making of both ends to meet, would be lessened if more money were in circulation, and that it would be easy to pay off mortgages if government should supply a plenty of silver. But excepting the proposition to lend directly to needy land-owners, a proposition to be defeated by the vote of everybody else, no one has found a channel through which silver can be made to flow from the national treasury into the pockets of the men who most loudly demand it.

Bankruptcy laws are provided for the benefit of insolvent debtors, enabling them to make new starts in life. Free coinage is advocated for the benefit of debtors generally, but where is there a solvent debtor who would not insist that he should be classed among creditors or among property-owners, rather than among debtors? A owns a farm and stock worth $15,000, and mortgaged for $10,000; B has a business, the balance-sheet of which, on one side, shows merchandise on hand worth $15,000, and on the other, debts amounting to $10,000; C has credits for $15,000, and debts for $10,000. In a short space of time, and in the ordinary course of events, each one of these individuals may so change his position as to have $5,000 in the bank, and be free of all debt. Before the change is made, will you insist that A belongs to "the debtor class," and that B or C does not? Alter the figures as you like, keeping the balance on the right side so that you do not bring in the insolvent debtors, and you will find that every debtor is more properly a creditor or a property-owner than a debtor. Search where you will, and yet you cannot find a "Debtor Class."

Gold bullion, gold money, silver money, and paper money, are each of them worth about thirty per cent.[1] more than *silver bullion* is worth; but it is not proposed that A, B, and C shall be permitted to collect in, or to sell for, gold bullion, gold money, silver money, and paper money, and be permitted at the same time to pay off debts in *silver bullion*. If sales or col-

[1] In 1896, say ninety per cent.

lections could be made for or in one of the four more valuable things, and at the same time debts be paid off with the less valuable thing, then debtors would be benefited, excepting that most debtors would be obliged first to collect in the less valuable thing in order to obtain the means of making their own payments. Carrying this absurdity a little farther, and referring to the A, B, and C already introduced, we may see that a law which should permit the payment of debts in *silver bullion* might possibly enable A to pay off $10,000 of debt with only about $7,700 of real money; enable B to do as well; but compel C to lose about $1,150, for C, instead of having a balance of $5,000 in money, would have a balance of $5,000 in *silver bullion*, worth only $3,850. Absurd as would be a proposition to benefit some debtors in this way, it becomes more ridiculous if you stop to consider that neither A nor B would be likely to be really benefited, for each one, in order to obtain the means for paying his debts, would be obliged to sell his farm or his merchandise for *silver bullion,* for if people could pay debts with *silver bullion*, most people would use it when buying farms or merchandise. A, B, and C, of course, would all suffer from the financial disturbance, due to the passage of such a foolish law.

This is not the proposed law, but the idea is to benefit debtors by making silver bullion worth about thirty per cent. more than it is now worth, or by bringing the purchasing power of money down to the purchasing power of silver bullion, or, what is the same thing, advancing prices about thirty per cent. It is claimed, for instance, that A's farm, which is now worth $15,000, can be made to be worth, say $19,000 to $20,000, and that the mortgage of $10,000 will then represent about one half instead of, as at present, two thirds of the value of the farm. B, it is claimed, would be able to sell his merchandise for $19,000 to $20,000, instead of for $15,000, and be able to realize a balance of $9,000 to $10,000, instead of $5,000. C, being so unfortunate as to have all his assets in credits, would be obliged to lose something like $1,150 in the *purchasing power* of his $5,000 balance.

B is the merchant or store-keeper, and if free coinage should advance prices he would obtain more for his stock of goods, but the money which he would accumulate would be worth less than money is now worth. In all probability, however, the financial disturbance would interfere with the free selling of merchandise. Banks would not so willingly lend money, because of the necessity to take depreciated, or further depreciated money, in settlement of loans, and if we reflect upon the enormous power of banking facilities in the making of prices, we shall see that our merchants and store-keepers are not in the way to be benefited by any cheapening of money, and this is true, whether our friend B or our friend C be considered typical "debtors." And certainly any benefit derived by either A or B would disappear if he should be in a similar situation when the United States should endeavor to return to the gold basis. Any good results possible to A or B from reducing the value of money would be matched by bad results to the A or B of the future, for the United States would as surely try to get back to the gold basis, as it did try to get back to that basis from the paper basis of 1862–1879.

Farmer A is the only "debtor" who is at all likely to be benefited by money-cheapening, and even he is not likely to be benefited unless his mortgage have some years to run. Promptness in the monetary change and avoidance of financial disturbance are requisite to enable most debtors to reap any benefit, but farmer A could hope that during the years which his mortgage has to run, the country would overcome the financial shock; and that his farm would be salable for $19,000 or $20,000, when his mortgage of $10,000 should fall due. If it should become clear before the mortgage falls due, that we are drifting upon a silver basis, then in renewing the mortgage farmer A would be obliged to agree to a "gold clause" in the contract, forcing him to pay gold or its equivalent in settlement of the mortgage. When we shall arrive at the time for the enacting of a free-coinage law, the number of farmer A's that could possibly reap a benefit from the law will be very small. Mortgagees may be trusted to take care of themselves, if given a reasonable time to do so.

Failure to notice that most debtors can as properly be classed with creditors, has led nations into adopting measures for the benefit of the former at the expense of the latter. Trade has been checked, borrowers have been prevented from obtaining new loans, and the uniform result of such unwise measures has been injury to nearly everybody. And to-day, in so far as the danger of our slipping off the gold basis is thought to be real, both European and American capitalists are avoiding long-time American loans or are insisting upon the "gold-clause" in long-time contracts. The industries of the country have already suffered enormously, because investors fear financial disturbance and because money-lenders and capitalists do not feel sure that borrowers will be able to return as good money as they wish to borrow; and, I have no doubt that farmer A's farm is worth, to-day, somewhat less than it would be worth if farm-buyers were fully assured that the valuable kind of money, which must now be used in purchasing a farm, could be obtained, when selling a farm, some years hence.

Undoubtedly there are individuals who stand ready to profit by the unlimited issue of silver money, or paper money, but of these individuals few are debtors and the total number is small. The mass of the people are always in position to be injured by any governmental folly, and have already been greatly injured by the mere talk or prospect of free coinage.

I do not consider it necessary to say that only dishonest people would favor the benefiting of debtors at the expense of creditors. Those people may have never considered the real composition of the so-called "debtor class," and may never think of debtors excepting as down-trodden individuals, although naturally debtors must be, as a rule, persons who are so fortunate so to possess standing or credit in the community. Then there are people who believe that "demonetization" took place; that the government thereby put prices down; that the fall in prices was more harmful than beneficial; and therefore that the government is able and ought to put prices up again. Lack of familiarity with the facts and with the actual workings and actual conditions of trade and finance does not imply lack of honesty.

Governmental action to advance prices—that is, to reduce the value of money—is unfair to all creditors who are not debtors, or are not to so great an amount. Wage-earners, salary-earners, pensioners, savings-bank depositors, the beneficiaries of life-insurance companies, and nearly all persons who receive fixed sums, or who are to receive money, the sum of which is already named, would be injured by an advance in the prices of commodities for the purchase of which that money must be used.

1896. During the past three years, unhappily, debtors and would-be borrowers have felt the evils of financial disturbance, and the very reverse of amelioration, coming from free-coinage talk. Debt-paying and debt-rearranging are always with us. Debt-scaling opportunity, through free-coinage of silver, is the dream of the politician, unrealizable at present, probably unrealizable in time for present debtors.

CHAPTER VII.

"THE BALANCE OF TRADE."—FOREIGN EXCHANGE.

TRADE is said to be "favorable" when the country's exports of merchandise exceed the imports. Trade is said to be "unfavorable" when the country's imports of merchandise exceed the exports. In the former case the *balance* of trade, so-called, is "favorable," and in the latter "unfavorable"; and so strongly is speculation affected either way by the knowledge of a "favorable" or "unfavorable" balance, that the market value of stocks often moves in obedience to this knowledge, so far that millions and millions of dollars are transferred from some pockets to others. We shall see, however, that this great power of "the balance of trade" is unwarranted,—is due, in fact, to a misunderstanding of the subject. It appears to be commonly supposed that a favorable balance of trade must be offset by importations of gold, and that for an unfavorable balance we must necessarily send gold out of the country. But the gold-movement itself, whether governed by trade conditions or not, generally attracts more attention than it deserves; at least so the writer hopes to prove.

The par of exchange[1] between America and England, therefore between America and the world, because of the world's custom of settling in London accounts between the traders of different countries, is 4.867, which means that £1 sterling is equivalent to $4.867 in gold; and whenever the market rate of exchange is at or close to this figure, no important quantity of gold can move between England and America either way, for the simple reason that it costs something to move the metal, say for freight, insurance, and to cover the

[1] The reader who would like to acquaint himself fully with the theory and practice of foreign exchanges should obtain *The Theory of the Foreign Exchanges*, by the Right Hon. George J. Goschen, M.P., although the book was written before the present par of exchange was established.

loss of interest while the gold is on the ocean. At this moment there are weekly arrivals of gold from Europe, and the market quotation for sterling exchange is about one per cent. below par. Perhaps a clipping from a daily paper[1] will serve to explain the situation :

"The par of sterling exchange is 4.867. The rate of demand sterling bills at which gold can be exported to London without loss is 4.88⅞ for bars, and 4.89¼ for coin, and the rate at which it can be imported without loss is 4.83¾.

"The market for sterling was firmer in tone in the forenoon, and 60 day rate advanced ⅛ cent at 12:11 P.M. Posted rates now 4.80½ and 4.84. The rates for actual business were as follows, viz.: Sixty days, 4.79¾; demand, 4.83¼; cables, 4.83¾ to 4.84. Commercial bills were 4.78½ to 4.78¾. The supply of cotton bills was fair."

Let us go over this in detail, considering the balance of trade when "favorable." The New York bankers whose business it is to carry on the financial part of foreign

---

[1] The New York *Evening Post*, October 13, 1891.

trade have such a strong desire for gold that for every pound sterling deliverable by their correspondents in London, on cable order, they are willing to accept, here, $4.83¾ to $4.84; for every pound sterling deliverable there, on demand, they would accept, here, $4.83¼; and for every one deliverable there, after the lapse of sixty days, these bankers would accept, here and now, $4.79¾, the bankers making interest in the meantime. Or we may say that the London correspondents of the New York bankers feel an unusually heavy demand for London bills of exchange drawn against New York, and have instructed the New York bankers to provide themselves with the money necessary to meet these bills. In the same newspaper paragraph we learn that there was a fair supply of cotton bills (a portion of the mass of commercial bills) and that commercial bills were worth only $4.78½ to $4.78¾ for each £1 sterling, which means that whoever, in America, at that moment, was in the act of making a sale of cotton, wheat, petroleum, or other product, to a buyer in any foreign country, would have to lose the difference between $4.78¾ and $4.867 upon each £1 sterling, the banker's profit included, less the interest from the date of selling his bill of exchange to the date of maturity of the bill. This is the state of affairs when it is said that the balance of trade is "favorable." In reality, when gold comes this way under these favorable conditions, the cost of bringing it must be borne, largely, by our exporters of merchandise, for when they ship goods they draw commercial bills of exchange against the foreign receivers of those goods and these bills of exchange must be sold to bankers who are already heavily loaded with similar bills of exchange.

If, when the balance of trade is "favorable," you should go to a banker and ask him for money to cover the value of merchandise which you were then exporting, he could rightly say: "So many exporters want to obtain money, just now, that I cannot supply them without fetching the money from England, and each exporter must pay his share of the necessary expense.

Your commercial bill of exchange must be cashed in London, at maturity, and the money must be shipped to New York, for that is the way at present to reimburse me." When, therefore, the balance of trade is "favorable" to this country our exporters, finding it difficult or expensive to obtain cash for their bills of exchange, contract their buying of exportable merchandise and force down the price of it, thus passing along to the farmer and the manufacturer a portion of the burden of expense entailed by the fetching of gold from Europe to America. Even if in adjusting the prices of goods to the point where exportation is possible, the expense of transporting gold be fastened partly upon the foreign buyers of the merchandise, still this expense is a tax upon our export business.

In regard, now, to our *import* business when the balance of trade is "favorable." At such a time European bankers will pay high rates for commercial bills of exchange drawn against New York, for by buying these bills and sending them to the bankers' New York correspondents these latter will be put in position to obtain here the money which we have seen to be in so great demand. Shippers of goods to America will find that, in addition to receiving the agreed-upon price for their goods, they possibly may receive a premium upon the bill of exchange drawn against the consignees of those goods, or, at least, receive the par value of their bills. When trade is "favorable" to this country, foreign shippers to America will be encouraged by this advantage, and may lower their prices to American buyers to induce them to buy more largely.

We thus see that when the balance of trade is "favorable" there are forces at work which both check the exportation of merchandise and encourage the importation of merchandise; and, on the other hand, we might as easily show that whenever the balance of trade is "unfavorable" there must be forces at work which check the importation of merchandise and encourage the exportation of merchandise. There are forces always at work which, sooner or later, bring about an equilibrium, only, however, to be overturned in due course, the processes of change going on indefinitely. When gold comes to us, or goes from us, we can hardly say that trade is "favorable" or "unfavorable," but, rather that trade *has been* favorable or unfavorable, and that powerful influences are at work in re-establishing the equilibrium.

But we may use the proper tense and still be far from understanding the broad subject of foreign exchange. The balance of trade is only one of many factors, for our exports of merchandise may exceed our imports of merchandise during a long period and yet no gold be sent to us. Evidently other things come into the calculation, and first let us note that it is not the balance of trade which should attract attention, but the balance of indebtedness. Europe can contract debts to America by the purchase of stocks, bonds, or other securities as readily as by the purchase of wheat, cotton, or petroleum, the rate of foreign exchange being similarly affected, no matter what Europe buys. Conversely, European owners of American securities when sending them to America obtain the right to draw against the American receivers of those securities. By the mediation of the bankers, one hundred shares of stock, worth $10,000, sent by a London firm to a New York firm, will make as much exchange against New York as ten thousand bushels of wheat, worth $10,000, shipped by a New York firm to a Liverpool firm, will make against London for Liverpool account. If the wheat and the stock transactions take place at the same time, and are represented by bills of exchange, maturing at the same time, one must offset the other; and it follows that a country's exports of merchandise may exceed its imports of merchandise, its balance of trade being called "favorable," and yet no balance of indebtedness appear, indebtedness for merchandise possibly balancing indebtedness for both stocks and merchandise. Important distinctions between securities and merchandise should be noted, however. As a rule, any kind of merchandise moves either to or from America, no kind, generally speaking, moving both ways; we exporting wheat, for instance, never importing it, and importing coffee, not exporting it; while, on the contrary, an identical bond or certificate of stock may cross the ocean many times. Then, the movement of merchandise is recorded, while the movement of securities is not recorded. Here is a tremendous force, this movement of securities, always at work but never measurable, sometimes offsetting the balance of trade and sometimes running with it, sometimes preventing importations or exportations of gold, and sometimes making necessary a larger volume of importation or exportation of the metal. Indeed, the activity of arbitrage brokers, buying and selling in the London and New York stock markets at the same moment, gives a mastering energy to this force. The close connection between gold movements and security movements may be more clear if we bear in mind that when a London banker wishes to pay gold to a New York banker he can order the latter to sell stock in New York, and borrow the stock for delivery there in order to bridge over the time taken by the London stock to reach New York.

Speaking now of a balance of indebtedness instead of a balance of trade, the indebtedness arising both from trade movements and security movements, a further complication shows itself: given the fact of indebtedness, the influx or efflux of gold will depend upon the character of that indebtedness, exactly as in every debtor's case the note which is due must be provided for, while the note which has some months to run may be put out of mind, the former requiring the use of ready money, the latter requiring only that business shall run along in the usual manner; or as a demand note must be provided for when payment is wanted, not when payment is not wanted. And between nations, as between individuals, the question of wanting or not wanting payment is determined by the rate of interest and the estimate placed upon the value of the security, and also upon the creditor's own financial position. As a matter of fact, we should remark here that because of the comparative newness of our country and the enterprising spirit of our people, we are a debtor as distinguished from a creditor nation, and corresponding with the usually high rate of interest prevailing in America, as judged by European standards, is the circumstance that this country is a great producer of securities. Those stocks and bonds which cross and recross the ocean are always American stocks and bonds, nobody here wanting any other. The sum total of them in European hands is unknown, but it probably exceeds our national debt.

The rate of foreign exchange, affected by trade movements and by the movements of securities, is also affected by interest and dividend payments and by remittances for freight on importations of merchandise, the owners of vessels usually being foreigners. Interest, dividend, and freight remittances make exchange as readily as movements of securities or merchandise make exchange. But for the necessity to continually buy bankers' bills of exchange against London, in order to pay, there, interest, dividend, and freight money, the rate of exchange would oftener fall to the gold-importing point, or would be more generally below the gold-exporting point, unless this effect were counteracted. It seems best to put in this proviso as a tribute to the vastness and complexity of the subject.

American securities owned abroad are of various kinds—bonds principal and interest payable in gold or payable in currency; bonds of defunct companies and bankrupt States, principal and interest doubtful or worse; income bonds, the principal payable in gold or payable in currency, the payment of interest doubtful; stocks of railroads, of other transportation companies, and of many industrial corporations, dividends doubtful or not, as each case may be, but *the principal not payable at all*, at least not by the issuer of such stocks. A bond is evidence of debt, specifying the interest, stating when the principal shall be paid, and naming either gold or legal money; a certificate of stock is evidence that the owner is a part-owner in the corporation, not a creditor of the corporation; and, having no right to regain his money except by sale of the stock, or the winding up of the corporation, such owner of stock, whether living in America or in Europe, necessarily takes the chance of finally receiving gold or currency, or more or less of either. Important to each party interested, as is the difference between bonds and stocks, the distinction is unimportant from our present point of view, so long as we consider the bonds and stocks which have a quotable value on both sides of the ocean. A corporation may pay no attention to its bonds which are to fall due twenty years hence, and may care not at all whether its stock sells on the market at a high price or a low price, and the officers of such corporation may not even know whether most of the bondholders and stockholders are Americans or Europeans; but every sale in London for American account, and every sale in New York for European account, affects directly the rate of foreign exchange between New York and the rest of the world.

Foreign exchange is affected too by the difference which exists, at any time, between the American and the European market rate of interest. If money can be loaned at ten per cent. in New York while only four per cent. can be obtained in London, there is an advantage in keeping money here, and London owners of loanable funds will instruct their New York correspondents to that effect; and, at such difference in rate, if continuing long enough, it would be well for London owners of loanable funds to send them to New York, the benefit of high interest more than offsetting the expense of transportation.

The fact of ours being a gold-producing country is quite important, for it indicates that a small annual exportation of gold should be expected.

The American habit of travelling abroad also has to do with the rate of exchange, many more Americans travelling there, than foreigners travelling here, and the means of supporting these Americans being drawn from here. Those of our countrymen who live abroad and draw their living from America, we may class with the great number of Europeans who own American securities.

We have now considered the factors in foreign exchange, but only under normal conditions and not in an exhaustive manner. Taking a limited view, we may say that whenever the market rate of demand, or cable, sterling bills (bankers') is much above 4.867, there is evidence of the existence of one or more of the following circumstances; foreign goods have been imported too freely, American goods are not wanted abroad, American securities find a better market here than in Europe, our rate of interest is too low to attract or keep foreign money, foreigners are short of money, much money is wanted abroad by American travellers, we have produced a surplus of gold, freight remittances are large, or interest and dividend payments on securities owned abroad are unusually heavy. And we may say that whenever the market rate of demand sterling bills is below 4.867, the reverse is true. Consequently when the rate has advanced to 4.88⅞, or has fallen to 4.83¾, the forces named must have been acting together in one or the other direction, or one or more of the forces must have been acting with overmastering energy. But whatever the force, or however great its energy, the opposing force always stops it, sooner or later, and the expense of moving gold across the ocean generally operates as a check upon the too powerful force. Ordinarily gold importations or gold exportations mean little more than that a tax has been laid upon those individuals who persist in doing business in one direction, after too much business has already been done in that direction. Almost every transatlantic shipment of gold indicates a derangement of our foreign business, but so nearly invariably of a temporary nature that the general public need pay little attention to it. As a matter of fact, I believe that since the resumption of specie payments in 1879, this country has neither gained nor lost, as the net result of importation and exportation, in any year, a sum of gold great enough to warrant half the variation in speculative prices which has been supposed to have resulted from such gain or loss of the metal. I am referring only to actual gain or loss of gold, not to, for instance, a downward movement in prices when brought about by fear that great quantities of gold *will be* exported to pay for American securities, this fear being based upon a belief that foreigners want to get rid of such securities.

NOTE TO THIRD EDITION.—When the currency became positively redundant after the crisis of 1893, the exportations of gold quite properly caused great fear of results, for a premium on gold was actually in sight. It seemed possible that gold money would become merchandise.

CHAPTER VIII.

FOREIGN EXCHANGE UNDER NORMAL AND UNDER ABNORMAL CONDITIONS.

This country does much of its business upon borrowed capital, but unfortunate as is the situation, it is not nearly so bad as would be the situation if we were unable to borrow or if our power of borrowing were curtailed. The merchant who, from large profits, pays a small portion for interest may well look upon his good credit as a very good thing; and Americans who bewail the sending of interest and dividend moneys to foreigners should console themselves with the thought that these payments are only a small portion of the total earnings on the capital which has been invested by foreigners in America. Nobody has any right to object to the benefit derived by us from our high credit abroad. When an American security is taken by a foreigner, the fact indicates that American capital can be employed to better advantage, and the fact of there being held abroad an enormous mass of American securities, indicates the release of an enormous sum of American capital for more profitable uses. Eastern capital is extensively used in the Western and Southern States, both because it cannot be so profitably used at home, and because the Westerners and Southerners can make a profit by its use in excess of the interest and dividends sent to Eastern capitalists. European capital is extensively used in the United States, both because it cannot be so profitably used at home, and because the people of the United States can make a profit by its use in excess of the interest and dividends sent to European capitalists.

Turning now to our lack of ownership in the steamers and sailing-vessels engaged in foreign trade, we may say that *under existing laws and circumstances* American capital is better employed. Without admitting that our merchant marine could not be restored, we may class freight money with interest and dividend money—all evidences that this country has not yet accumulated sufficient capital for all its business wants.

The newness of America, her immense resources, and the honesty, inventive genius, and enterprising character of the people have drawn hither foreign capital, and should continue to draw it. Therefore we may class as a normal factor in foreign exchange the flow of foreign capital this way for investment; and, consequently, we may also class among the normal factors in foreign exchange the flow toward Europe of interest and dividend disbursements, leaving questionable the classification of freight remittances, but bearing in mind that such remittances are continually being made. Intimately connected, we may note here, are capital and its earnings, and there can be no doubt that the greater the interest and dividend payments to foreigners the larger will be the total of foreign capital invested; and, naturally, the greater the earnings of vessels engaged in American foreign trade, the larger will be the sum of such investments.

Looking upon the purchasing of American securities by foreigners as the natural condition of our present attainment in growth, so to speak, we may consider the selling of American securities by foreigners to Americans as quite abnormal. The home-coming of our stocks and bonds should resemble an eddy in a stream, and should not resemble the stream itself. When those stocks and bonds move this way in large volume, something, certainly, is the matter; and, of course, several forces may have worked together to reverse the natural movement of the stream. We may do well to note some of these forces. The expectation of the failure of a great house, and the actual failure of the Barings in London, in 1890, by creating a very great demand for money, induced many sales of American securities to Americans, and these sales were like a creditor's demands for money. But a flow of American securities this way, brought about by a shortage of money in London, should be distinguished from a similar flow of American securities when it is caused, not by any trouble among our creditors, but by their *fear* that we intend to commit an act detrimental to their interests. In 1890 and in 1891 many sales of securities for shipment to America were made because the owners needed money, and many, doubtless, were made because the owners expected that pro-silver legislation here would be "discounted" by a fall in our stock market and by a decline in the activity of most of our industries. In European eyes, free silver coinage would be supreme folly; therefore the wisdom of selling American securities long before such an act could be passed,—in common parlance, the wisdom of "discounting" the future. And at the same time that foreign holders of American securities are frightened into selling, would-be foreign investors in American securities are deterred from buying, for if a European wish to sell stock now because he can obtain $10,000 in gold, and because he thinks he may be able to obtain in the future only $10,000 in silver, gold money then to be worth thirty per cent. more than silver money;' so, in the same manner, a would-be investor in American stock could reason that by holding $10,000 in gold until the American gold money shall be worth thirty per cent. more than the American silver money, he will be able first to give $10,000 in gold for $13,000 in silver, then use $10,000 of the silver in purchasing the stock, and be able to retain $3,000 as a profit for waiting. In the first half of the year 1891 we exported about $73,000,000 in gold, coin and bars, and in the second half of the same year we imported only about $38,000,000, in spite of the fact that in the second half of the year the natural return movement was assisted by a phenomenal circumstance, viz.: crops were very short abroad and were very abundant here. The general expectation in the summer of 1891 that most of the $73,000,000 would come back, was disappointed, I believe, because European owners of American securities and European would-be investors had imbibed a fear of American pro-silver legislation. Lack of

[1] Say ninety per cent. in 1896.

accurate knowledge in Europe of our affairs results in great weight being given to the speeches of American Senators and Representatives. Without doubt, I think we may say that in the year 1891 abnormal conditions kept foreign exchange up to the gold-exporting point for a much longer time than it otherwise would have remained there; and I think the principal abnormal condition was the absence of desire in Europe to hold or to buy American securities. If we are bent upon free coinage, Europe would best await the result, and most assuredly it would be best for Europe to allow us to carry our own stocks, for stocks are representative of legal money only, whatever that may be. Many European capitalists fully believe that, do what we will, we have now gone so far in the direction of the silver basis that we cannot avoid arriving there; and naturally these capitalists, at least, can see no advantage in holding American stocks.[1] I confess to some sympathy with my countrymen who in answer to all this would say: Let Americans hold their own stocks and bonds

---

[1] In 1894, '95, '96, the **actual arrival** at the silver basis was avoided **only by** bond issuing.

and we shall be free from this troublesome indebtedness to foreigners. It certainly would be better if we could hold them, but unfortunately we cannot. Our position is like that of a man who has a special partner. The special partner draws a share of the profits, but does no work, and the man who does the work feels a desire to keep all the profits. If, however, he be a sensible fellow, he will not act in a way that shall lead to the special partner's *refusing to remain* in the business, the only sensible course to pursue being to accumulate so much money that the special partner shall not be needed. As a nation, our sensible course is to use whatever sum of foreign capital we need and can get in the development of our industries, and to treat the owners of this capital as we should treat assistants, not as we should treat enemies. We can hope for the good time when we shall have accumulated a sufficiency of capital of our own for all of our wants, but until we do obtain this ownership, braggadocio is unwarranted. Our true interest lies in so acting that foreigners will buy American securities and will keep them *until we want them.* No true American interest can be served by teaching foreigners that our securities are not good securities, that the appearance of gold value may turn into the reality of silver value.

The abnormal factor in foreign exchange, the home-coming of American securities, is connected with another abnormal factor, the forcible holding of the rate of interest below the proper rate. Profits and wages in this country are higher, on the average, than they are in Europe, and, as naturally, interest should be higher too. When, therefore, Congress tries to make money plentiful it is apt to create an abnormal factor in foreign exchange, and when Congress succeeds in its efforts this abnormal factor in foreign exchange operates to *send gold out of the country.* In our present state of development, the use of money here ought to be valued more highly than the use of money abroad, and we have seen that the rate of foreign exchange is forced down toward the gold-importing point and away from the gold-

---

[1] The surplus of money in 1894 was the principal factor in foreign exchange at that time.

exporting point by our comparatively high rate of interest. Make money too plentiful, then, and you take away one of the inducements for foreigners to leave money here; and the only money which they will take away is gold money. Issue too much silver or silver notes and you both make money too cheap and create a fear of the proximity of the silver basis. It is true that no governmental issues of money can hold down permanently the rate of interest, but the first effect is to make money plentiful, and therefore to cause exportation of the kind of money that foreigners want.

If the issue of new money should have the effect of putting prices up, or of holding them above the normal level, there would necessarily be a still stronger tendency in gold to leave the country. Foreign exchange would be kept at the gold-exporting point, because Americans were buying or holding too large quantities of stocks, bonds, or merchandise. When new issues of money are absorbed by the people, the absorption *can have* a very bad effect in fostering speculation, and *if* it have this effect the inevitable collapse is sure to be disastrous, in a degree proportionate to the height of the speculation fever. But it must not be assumed that new issues of money *necessarily* affect prices. Indeed, when prices are affected, the circumstances are peculiar, as we shall see in Chapter XII., on *The Old Volume of Money Theory.*

Gresham's law, under which "a cheaper or depreciated currency always tends to displace a more valuable one,"[1] should be studied carefully, because, in our case, gold slips away so easily. If we put the rate of interest below the level which suits the conditions of trade, if we create or foster a feeling among foreign buyers or holders of American securities that a foolish financial policy is likely to be adopted, we inevitably move the rate of foreign exchange up to the gold-exporting point, or we keep the rate above the normal rate, that rate which would prevail if these abnormal factors were not affecting it. Gold may

[1] *The Principles of Political Economy*, Simon Newcomb, Ph.D., LL.D.

be actually exported, or the importations of gold which otherwise would take place may be prevented, but, as in the course of a year gold generally moves both ways across the ocean, the net loss in a year, from bad financial laws, must be felt. At some future time, perhaps, we may do very well without foreign financial assistance, but at present it certainly would be wise for legislators to fully acquaint themselves with the actual workings of foreign exchange.

I do not think it requires any argument to prove that foreign exchange cannot be held at the gold-exporting point for a very long time without Americans seeing the inevitable consequence, and seeing the propriety of securing for themselves the coming premium on gold.

NOTE TO THIRD EDITION.—In 1893, '94, '95, American hoarding of gold was very strongly stimulated by gold exportation. Gold exportation was caused to some extent by an unusual factor, that of certain governments paying a premium on gold or **paying** the loss indicated in the current rate of exchange.

CHAPTER IX.

DISCUSSION WITH REPRESENTATIVE ADVOCATES OF SILVER.[1]

Mr. H——, who favors American silver exclusively, finds no difficulty in answering the champion of all silver, Senator Stewart; but the difference between the two gentlemen appears to be only in degree, and I think it fair to call it lucky for them that they are not proposing to run their own affairs in the manner suggested by them for the United States. Apologizing to these gentlemen for being personal, the importance of the subject leads me to ask: Would not Senator Stewart's friends clap him into an asylum,

---

[1] In the summer of 1891, the New York *Evening Telegram* opened its columns to a general discussion of the silver question. The author's part in that discussion is reproduced here, after careful revision, and with many additions. He has not been so anxious to avoid repeating himself as he would have been if the silver question were less important, and he believes that reiteration is sometimes in order.

and would not Mr. H—— sooner or later be placed out of harm's way?

The Senator suggests the free coinage of all silver, and this means that the United States should buy, at $1.29 an ounce, the world's stock or surplus of what it values at less than $1 an ounce.[1] As a rule, sane people do not pay more than the market price of anything and do not try to change the world's market price at the expense of their own pockets.

Let us see what would happen if the Senator should have his way. The fact that there is an immense surplus of silver in the world is proved by there having been a great increase in production and a great decline in market price; and if there is not enough silver for the United States to draw upon there are surely plenty of mines which at higher market prices could produce any lacking quantity. If now we pay $1.29 per ounce that price would become the market price, but only at the point of delivery to the United States Mint. At all other points the bullion dealers would necessarily fix the price at $1.29 per

[1] Less than seventy cents in 1896.

ounce, less the cost of carriage to the United States Mint, and less a fair profit for the risk that the United States might see its own folly and stop buying silver before delivery could be made. The world's dealers in bullion know the amount of gold in the Treasury of the United States and know that European governments are anxious to obtain gold and to get rid of silver. The problem for the bullion dealers would be: How long can or will the United States take silver and pay out gold? The questions in the United States would be: How quickly can we stop taking the world's silver and giving the world our gold, and what adequate punishment can be inflicted upon Senator Stewart and his friends? And, reading of the Senator's being hanged in effigy all over the United States by patriotic small boys, the world's bullion dealers would hurry on their silver and would reduce their purchases of it. The market price of silver, therefore, would never quite reach the Treasury price of $1.29 per ounce.

All this is clear to Mr. H—— and so he wants us to buy American silver only, still at $1.29 per ounce, although American silver is worth no more in the world's markets than any other silver. If this idea should prevail, the question with American miners would be: How much can we increase our production and how much silver can we deliver at the Mint before the government shall see the need to stop buying?

I may be pardoned for saying just here that it was hardly necessary for Mr. H—— to state that he is engaged in silver-mining. And I would ask if he would guarantee that Mexican silver shall not be carried to American mines and thence to the United States Mint? Does he propose that Treasury officials shall keep watch over every hole in American ground to prevent it being stocked with Mexican silver and then developed into an American silver mine?

Will he furnish to the Treasury, experts who are capable of telling the difference between American and foreign silver? Is there a distinguishable difference?

If, to stop importations, Mr. H—— would tax importations of silver, how would he avoid taxing such silver as had been previously exported, and, would not his law violate the constitution which prohibits the taxing of any article exported from any State? Importers of silver, in order to avoid the paying of duty upon it, would claim that their particular lots of silver were American silver and therefore exempt from taxation.

Surely common sense has a place in this discussion, and the silver men should be willing to allow the United States to buy as cheaply as possible, for in this way the United States can buy about one third more in quantity,[1] to say nothing of the fact that this way would be more fair to all taxpayers who must pay for the purchases. It has been shown by years of trying to make silver circulate, that Americans will not carry much silver in their pockets and cannot be induced to do so; and it can be assumed that the silver which the government takes, it will be obliged to pile up on top of its already enor-

[1] 1896. Nearly twice the quantity.

mous stock, and will be obliged to hold until such time as it sees fit to sell to the world and at the world's price. The higher the price, too, which the government pays for silver, the greater will be the stimulation to silver-mining all over the world, unless the government should quickly obtain all it could pay for, or quickly abandon its position of buyer.

Free coinage, or what is the same thing, the paying of $1.2929 an ounce for a metal worth less than $1, would make us the world's laughing-stock, and European governments would vie with each other in the struggle to get our gold before we should be able to comprehend the point of the joke.

Somewhat farther away from lunacy is the present law,[1] by the operation of which the United States was changed from a silver exporting to a silver-importing or non-exporting country. Even paying only the market price the Treasury has shown itself to be the world's best buyer of silver, and according to the report of the Secretary of the Treasury, 1890, the natural flow of silver

[1] Repealed in 1893.

from the American mines to Oriental countries had been stopped. The Orientals who use silver for money, and exclusively, can get along with a diminished supply to accommodate the vaults of the United States Treasury, and is it to be supposed that the Orient can spare none of its stock if we offer to pay an advance of thirty per cent.? But the Orient does not want gold money and Europe does, and the question is, How much silver could Europe and the Orient and the rest of the world spare to fill our Treasury vaults?

If I understand Mr. Wm. P. St. John (New York *Evening Telegram*, August 15, 1891), he relies upon the fact that the European coinage parity of silver to gold is $15\frac{1}{2}$ to 1, whereas our coinage parity is 16 to 1, this difference making silver money abroad worth, nominally, about $1.33 per ounce, while here it is worth, nominally, $1.2929 per ounce. Mr. St. John argues that the silver money of Europe would not come here, under free coinage in this country, because we should then be offering to pay only $1.2929 per ounce for that which is worth at home $1.33 per ounce.

The Bank of France now holds the equivalent of about $260,000,000 in gold and of about $245,000,000 in silver. The market value of the gold as bullion is $260,000,000, but the market value of the silver is less than $171,500,000—say thirty per cent. lower than the nominal value. Suppose, now, that the United States government should say to the Bank of France: Give us $100,000,000 in silver and we will give you $97,000,000 in gold, or reduce your nominal valuation by three per cent., and we will give you gold which possesses actual value more than thirty per cent. greater. If Mr. St. John were a director in the Bank of France, he would vote *Nay*, and would contend that *market value* is of no consequence, *nominal value* being all that need be considered. But he would be outvoted, for some bright Frenchman would say: "Let us take the American gold, and after we get it we can, if we like, purchase silver at the market price. I think we should find ourselves in possession of much more silver than we have now, the *increase in quantity being the profit on the transaction.* Lose sight of coinage parity for a while and consider only market value. Sell silver at about thirty per cent. above the present market value, coin the incoming gold into napoleons and ten- and five-franc pieces, take any chances that the market value of silver will go up to $1.29 or $1.33 per ounce, and remain there; and when we get ready to do so and think it advisable to do so, we can begin to buy silver in such small quantities as absolutely needed, so as to get back in time an equivalent sum of silver at lowest market prices."

When Mr. St. John lends the money of his own bank upon securities, I presume that he takes into consideration the salable value of those securities, rather than the nominal value; and if he were a director in the Bank of France, I believe that he could be shown the advisability of losing three per cent. in the nominal value of the assets of the Bank, if by so doing the Bank could gain thirty per cent. in its real assets.

If it should be argued that free coinage here or unlimited purchase would put up the price of silver bullion, and the Bank of France thus would never be able to get back its silver, and would be obliged to lose the three per cent., still it must be admitted that a permanent advance in the price of silver bullion is at least doubtful, and even if the advance should prove to be permanent, the loss is only three per cent., while in the view of non-permanency of the advance the gain is thirty per cent. Who, as a director in the Bank of France, would not gladly vote to give in silver $100,000,000 or $200,000,000, *nominal value*, for $97,000,000 or $194,000,000 in gold, *both real and nominal* value?

If the reader will drop from his mind *parity of coinage*, as a good merchant sometimes dismisses a mere book-keeping question, in order to obtain a perfectly clear view of a subject, there need be no difficulty in seeing that should the Bank of

France sell 100,000,000 ounces of silver for $129,290,000, and later on, years later perhaps, should buy 100,000,000 ounces of silver for $100,000,000, the Bank will make a profit of $29,290,000. Or, on 200,000,000 ounces the profit would be $58,580,000.[1] It might well be reasoned that our buying of silver would so stimulate production that silver would in time go to a price lower than any yet recorded, or it might be considered good financiering to never buy back the silver at all, for so the Bank of France would be put in a position similar to that held by the Bank of England. In any case, the selling of 100,000,000 or 200,000,000 ounces of silver for 29 to 30 per cent. more than the market value, would be a wise thing to do; and I cannot think that it requires a strong imagination to picture even now a wily Gaul, quietly chuckling over the utterances of our St. Johns, our Stewarts, our Pughs, our Blands, and our Bartines, and hoping and praying that these men will succeed in giving him the one opportunity of his life for a brilliant *coup de finance*.

[1] **Say** $100,000,000 profit **in 1896.**

If, instead of free coinage or unlimited purchase, a measure were proposed to *try free coinage for one year,* scarcely anybody could fail to see that the world and the world's miners would send a fabulous quantity of silver to the Treasury in order to obtain $1.29 per ounce for a metal the value of which would be sure to fall to less than $1 per ounce as soon as the year had expired. And what reason is there to suppose that under a free-coinage law unlimited in time the financial men of the world, noticing the piling up of silver in the United States Treasury, would be unable to foresee that the law must in time be repealed?

The present price of silver is upheld by the Treasury's monthly purchase[1] of an amount about as great as the whole product of the American mines; and upheld, also, by the purchase of large quantities of silver for use in the arts, because of the comparatively low price of the metal. But if you drive manufacturers into the habit of using less silver, and if you fill the treasury so full that necessity or a

[1] **Stopped in** 1893.

revulsion in public sentiment shall shut up this dumping-hole, what then would be the market price of silver in the face of a phenomenally large production? No law can be passed which could not be repealed, and therefore the question for those engaged in the silver industry appears to be this: Would the profit of an advance in the price of silver for a short time cover the later loss of a heavy decline to last a very long time? What would be the market price of silver if, to get back to the gold basis, the United States Treasury, instead of buying 4,500,000 ounces of silver per month, should become a seller of silver? The quantity of silver which could be supplied to the Treasury by the world, assisted by the world's mines, at $1.29 per ounce, is unlimited; not so the amount which the world could be induced to take back at $1, or even 75 cents per ounce, if I may be allowed to guess at a figure.

Whoever has been interested in trying to corner a commodity, or has read of such attempts, like that, for instance, of the

Société des Metaux, in its trying to control the price of copper, must know that even the Treasury of the United States is not sufficiently powerful to hold up the price of silver. The visible supply is said to be a small amount, but the visible supply is nothing compared to the invisible supply, and if the United States should adopt free coinage or unlimited purchase, this question would inevitably present itself: Which can hold out the longer, the United States Treasury in receiving silver, or the bowels of the earth in delivering silver?

Note—The term *free coinage* is used in this volume in the American popular sense, indicating coining freely or to an unlimited extent. Seigniorage (minting charge) is not considered.

CHAPTER X.

THE DISCUSSION CONCLUDED.

I GLADLY apologize to Senator Stewart for seriously offending him (indicated in a newspaper letter by the Senator), and, in order to be sure of suiting the gentleman, I will now, so far as possible, use his own language. If he be involved in errors and inconsistencies he may charge the trouble to his being on the wrong side of the question. He need not consider the affair wholly personal. In this chapter quotation marks will be used only to designate the words of the distinguished Senator, extracts being made from the *Evening Telegram* of July 30, August 5, and August 18, 1891.

He claims to have "proved that the people of the United States could not be injured by free coinage," and alludes to " the impossibility of a flood of silver." The basis for this may be his statement as follows:

"The supply of gold and silver from the mines was more nearly equal at the time, and since silver was demonetized, than at any other period of which the record has been preserved. There was, in 1873, a little more gold produced in the world than silver. There has been since that time a little more silver produced than gold. But during the twenty-three years from 1850 to 1873 there was about three times as much gold produced as silver."

Here we have on Mr. Stewart's own authority proof of the *naturalness of the decline* in the value of silver, as distinct from the "demonetization" charge, which he is so fond of making. Up to 1873, on a very large production of gold and a very small production of silver, the ratio of 15½ to 1 was easily maintained; that is to say, on this parity of value, the production of each metal corresponded somewhat closely to the demand for each, the production of gold being "three times" as great as the production of silver.

But the production of silver has far exceeded the demand for it, and therefore the price has necessarily fallen. Note how the ratio of the world's production of the two metals has changed, as shown in the following table taken from the *Engineering and Mining Journal* of July 25, 1891, the figures being the United States coining value:[1]

	Gold.	Silver.
1855	132,000,000	40,000,000
1860	127,000,000	40,000,000
1865	126,000,000	52,000,000
1870	123,000,000	64,000,000
1875	111,000,000	82,000,000
1880	108,000,000	101,000,000
1881	104,000,000	106,000,000
1882	100,000,000	111,000,000
1883	97,000,000	115,000,000
1884	100,000,000	120,000,000
1885	106,000,000	125,000,000
1886	106,000,000	130,000,000
1887	106,000,000	136,000,000
1888	110,000,000	146,000,000
1889	120,000,000	159,000,000

If the annual production of silver were now equal only to one third the production of gold, or, say, perhaps, not over half as great as the production of gold, pos-

---

[1] 1896. The *coinage* values of the annual production of the two metals are now about equal—close to $200,000,000. The *market* value of the silver annually produced is about $100,000,000.

sibly, indeed, if the production of silver had not overtaken the production of gold, the old ratio of 15½ or 16 to 1 would be maintainable. In other words, if 15½ or 16 to 1 was the proper ratio when "three times as much gold" was produced as silver, then 15½ or 16 to 1 cannot possibly be the proper ratio to-day. The world's markets say that to-day's ratio is about 21 to 1,[1] and, in view of the figures above given, I do not see how Mr. Stewart can reasonably find fault with the world's opinion.

If we say that the growth of business demands an ever increasing supply of money, losing sight of the fact that banking facilities keep pace with business and largely supply its needs, making a dollar more and more important as a measure of value and less and less important as a means of exchange; or, if we say that an annually increasing crop of money is needed just as much as we need an annually increasing crop of wheat, losing sight of the fact that wheat is consumed while money is largely preserved, still we have no ground for assuming that there is any

[1] 1896. About 31 to 1.

need for the disproportionately great production of silver. On the contrary, the fall in the price of silver, from $1.29 per ounce to ninety-seven cents per ounce,[1] shows that no matter how badly the world needs money, it prefers all the evils of the shortage rather than the use of more silver. The worthy advocate of silver may insist that the world is mistaken in this choice, but certain it is that the world has made such a choice, else the parity of 15½ or 16 to 1 would never have changed to that of 21 to 1.[2]

Let me here make again the distinction between money and wealth, terms too frequently used as synonymous. There is always an insatiable demand for wealth, but the demand for money is limited, like the demand for a commodity. More closely limited, of course, is the demand for a kind of money upon which suspicion has been cast.

The whole world, however, does not take the same view of silver. It is good enough money yet for some countries, and there is left open to Senator Stewart the

---
[1] 18.6. About sixty-eight cents.
[2] Now about 31 to 1.

course of educating the people of Europe and the United States up to the standard of China, India,[1] Peru and Mexico! After all, a mere free-coinage or unlimited-purchase bill could have little effect upon the price of silver compared to such an effect as would come from teaching civilized people that they ought to carry the white metal and overlook its depreciation. Education strikes at the root of the evil; any act of Congress may be undone by a subsequent Congress!

In the column next to the one containing the Senator's assurance of an "impossibility of a flood of silver," August 18th, the newspaper said: Silver is top-heavy. (It was.) There is much talk of a flood of silver from over the water. Holland has 149,000,000 florins in the treasury for which there is no call in circulation. The Dutch and German ministers think they will take no more chances, but will sell their silver this year; and more news, or rumors, of this tenor. It is, of course, a matter of conjecture what European gov-

[1] Even in India free-coinage found its limit, and was stopped in 1893.

ernments will do, but it cannot be questioned that their actions for eighteen years indicate a strong desire to obtain gold and to give silver in exchange.¹

What European ministers say, is a question of policy, and if a government wish to give silver for gold that government's financial minister cannot be expected to say anything which would weaken the cause of free coinage or unlimited purchase in America. To get rid of silver he must have a market; to obtain gold he must have a source of supply. Under free coinage or unlimited purchase we should furnish both. Perhaps, however, Senator Stewart will be more easily convinced that there is a European demand for gold if I use his own words:

"I called attention to the fact that all the great monetary institutions in Europe and America, where the gold standard is maintained, were deficient in reserves to meet their obligations, and they were struggling for more gold and reducing credits to save themselves from bankruptcy."

¹ 1896. **Austria-Hungary is** accumulating gold, having decided upon gold resumption. **Silver has** proved burdensome.

Possibly Mr. Stewart may have been posing as a world's philanthropist, for in another place he said:

"We have already shown that gold would be cheaper in Europe if they had more of it, as they would have if they had all the gold in this country, and in that case he (the debtor) could get more gold for the same property than he now can, and could pay his debts with less sacrifice, no matter whether his debt was a gold obligation or an obligation to pay in the currency of the United States."

The benefit to Europe from having our gold is perfectly clear; not so the benefit to us from losing our gold, one third of our circulating medium, even if we could be summarily educated up to the belief that silver is just as good as gold.

The Senator says that if I "had taken the trouble to read" one of his articles I "would have been saved the trouble of many mistakes and erroneous statements with regard to paying $1.29 for a dollar's worth of silver." According to the Senator there is, then, an important, and not merely a technical, difference between free coinage and a policy of purchasing silver at $1.29 per ounce. But if he will admit that 480 grains make one ounce and also that the silver dollar contains $371\frac{1}{4}$ grains, then I do not see how he can escape from the truth of a simple equation: 480 times 1 equals $371\frac{1}{4}$ times 1.2929. He says: "Under the Bland act the government bought a large amount of silver bullion from the miners at the market price, coined it into silver dollars and paid it out for current expenses. By this transaction the director of the Mint informs us that the government made a clean profit of $70,000,000 between the market price of the bullion so purchased and the coin value of the silver dollar." And he also says: "Under the law of 1890, now in force,[1] the government does not buy silver with money raised by taxation, but issues Treasury notes for silver bullion at the market price, dollar for dollar. The silver bullion as received is deposited in the Treasury, and the Secretary is authorized by law to coin it into standard dollars. By doing

[1] Repealed in 1893.

so the government will make the difference between the market price of silver and the coin value, which is now about twenty-five per cent."

From the equation above given, from the fact that silver is worth about ninety-seven cents per ounce, and from the Senator's own words, is it not perfectly clear that the profit which the government makes is due wholly to our not having free coinage? Is it not certain that this profit, now owned by the whole people, represented by the government, would, under free coinage, have gone into the pockets of miners, bullion dealers, and speculators?

Under free coinage the government would take an unlimited amount of silver, and would give in exchange one dollar for every unit of $371\frac{1}{4}$ grains. Under a law which should provide for the purchase of an unlimited amount of silver at $1.2929 per ounce, the government would pay out a similar sum of money for a similar quantity of silver. Some free-coinage advocates themselves speak of free coinage as sure to raise the world's price of silver to $1.29 per ounce, but a technical difference is immensely important to Senator Stewart. And he is quite right, for if, instead of favoring free coinage he should favor the same thing, under a different name, say a bill to compel the United States Treasury to purchase the world's surplus stock of silver and the world's future surplus product of silver, at $1.29 per ounce, he would have no chance of success.

The nervousness of the silver advocates whenever free coinage is spoken of as equivalent to an unlimited purchase of silver at $1.2929 per ounce was instanced when Mr. Leech, the Director of the Mint, was examined by the House Committee on Coinage, Weights, and Measures, Fifty-first Congress:

"Mr. Taylor: Would free coinage make silver any more valuable provided there were no provision to compel the government to purchase the coin?

"Mr. Leech: Free coinage in this bill is in itself a purchase.

"Mr. Taylor: Not on the part of the government?

"Mr. Leech: Why, certainly. This is a bill for the free purchase of silver. Under the present law if we had free coinage it would be the same thing, because they would simply deposit their silver and get silver certificates.

"Mr. Taylor: Suppose they did not have that provision; they did not formerly have it; suppose that was stricken out?

"Mr. Leech: That would necessarily limit the output of silver dollars to the capacity of the mints to coin.

"Mr. Taylor: Would that increase the value of silver?

"Mr. Leech: I think it would.

"Mr. Walker: I should like to ask the Director whether he means by that, if this country alone granted free coinage that would of itself make the silver dollar and the gold dollar interchangeable in this country; simply granting free coinage at the present ratio of weights?

"Mr. Leech: It would make it interchangeable as long as we had gold dollars to interchange.

"Mr. Walker: How long do you think that would be?

"Mr. Leech: That depends on how much silver came here, and how many legal-tender notes were paid out in the purchase of it, and to what extent gold was hoarded or left the country. I do not think it would be very long.

"Mr. Vaux: Would it appreciate it or depreciate it?

"Mr. Leech: I think the effects of this bill¹ would be to attract to our mints large quantities of silver. I believe the current product of the world would naturally move here. In addition to that, I believe that European countries would avail themselves of this opportunity, which they believe cannot last, to get rid of their embarrassing stocks of silver and adopt the gold standard. I believe Austria-Hungary would resume specie payments on the gold basis. She cannot resume on the silver basis. I think they would avail themselves of this opportunity to convert their

¹ One of the many free-coinage bills.

silver coins into our full legal-tender money and get our gold for them even at a slight loss. I think other European countries would do the same. I think that is proven by the fact that European countries are doing that now, or, at least, seriously considering it.

  * * * * *

"Mr. Vaux: Does this bill provide that the government shall buy silver at a certain price?

"Mr. Leech: At a fixed price, $1.2929 per fine ounce.

  * * * * *

"Mr. Bland: Do you believe that under free coinage the government buys anything at all?

"Mr. Leech: Under this bill they would. I understand Mr. Bland's bill makes all the certificates full legal tender.

"Mr. Bland: I simply mean free coinage stripped of any certificates. I mean the naked question of free coinage stripped of any certificates. Do you believe that under free coinage the government buys anything at all?

"Mr. Vaux: The people do not give it to the government.

"Mr. Williams: How much does it cost the government every year?

"Mr. Bartine: Just what it costs to coin it.

"Mr. Bland: The government has no responsibilities after it is coined.

"Mr. Leech: Yes, sir; it requires that it shall be taken as full legal tender in the payment of all debts. The government does not simply coin it and stamp it.

"Mr. Bland: The government does not buy it and it is not responsible for it.

"Mr. Leech: The government is responsible for it.

"Mr. Bland: If it were it would keep it at par with gold.

"Mr. Leech: Why so?

"Mr. Bland: Because gold is the standard of value in the United States. Has not the Congress as much right to make silver the standard?

"Mr. Leech: Certainly.

"Mr. Bland: Is not Congress the representative of the people?

"Mr. Leech: Yes, sir.

"Mr. Bland: When you talk about the purchase of silver, where is the purchase on the part of the government any more than the purchase of gold?

"Mr Leech: We purchase gold now. We do not take gold and coin it for the people. That is the theory of the law. We give a man a check as soon as it is assayed. We would do the same with silver under your bill. I do not see any practical difference between free coinage and unlimited purchase of silver except one is a shorter method.

"Mr. Bland: That is discretionary with the depositor. The depositor has the right to wait until he gets his coin.

"Mr. Leech: He does not want to wait.

"Mr. Bartine: It is merely to obviate the necessity of waiting?

"Mr. Leech: Yes, sir.

"Mr. Walker: If I understand your statement, the government does purchase it. It amounts practically to a purchase.

"Mr. Bland: *I was asking as to laws and not as to opinions, or as to policies, or discretionary powers.*"

It would never do for Mr. Bland or Senator Stewart to admit that free-coinage of silver is equivalent to unlimited purchase of silver at $1.2929 per ounce, for American common-sense would oppose the purchasing of anything at thirty per cent. above its market value, but nevertheless the true meaning of free coinage will eventually be well understood.

1896. It is much better understood to-day, and of course the objection to paying about ninety per cent. above market value is stronger than the former objection to paying thirty per cent. above market value.

CHAPTER XI.

"ULTIMATE REDEMPTION."

Senator Stewart's argument is as follows:

"My reason for asserting that there is not gold enough for use as money I will again repeat. Statisticians inform us that in 1873 there were nearly $8,000,000,000 of real money of ultimate redemption, certainly over $7,000,000,000. The real money at that time which required no promise of redemption consisted of gold and silver coin. On the gold theory there is now less than one half as much money of ultimate redemption as there was eighteen years ago. The Director of the Mint informs us that there is only $3,727,000,000 of gold coin in the world, which, according to the gold advocates, is all the real money which now exists. If it required about $8,000,000,000 of coin as a basis of paper circulation and commercial credits eighteen years ago, I contended that less than one half of that amount was not enough to sustain the present fabric of business and credit."[1]

Redemption how, when, where, and by whom?

Is the real money in the world to be collected, piled up, and counted, and then doled out in exchange for the paper substitutes of all kinds which now pass from hand to hand and from country to country? Do people who now freely give valuable things for the bits of paper called Treasury-notes, bank-notes, checks, drafts, bills of exchange, etc., etc., do so with the mental reservation: This is all right for the present, but *some day* all these bits of paper must be redeemed in gold, or at least in equal parts of gold and silver? Is the time of "ultimate redemption" fixed for this year or next, or for some other year? Is the place of redemption London, New York, Hong Kong, or is this point not yet agreed upon? Is the duty of seeing that every owner of paper shall be given the

[1] New York *Evening Telegram*, 1891.

sum of money named on the face of the paper, a duty for our government or for some other government to perform, or shall redemption be performed by a congress of the world's financiers, representing the various nations in proportion to the sum of paper held by the traders of each country? And if the manner, the time, the place, the manager of "ultimate redemption" can not be named, then what folly it is to talk of "ultimate redemption"!

Actual redemption, however, there is all the time and everywhere and by everybody who continues solvent. Continuous redemption is familiar to all business men; "ultimate redemption" is a mere theory. A gives a check to B for $1,000, and he deposits it in bank; B gives a check to C for $1,000 and this check is deposited in another bank; C gives a similar check to D and this goes into still another bank; D gives two checks for $500 each to E and F, who deposit, respectively, in two more banks; E draws checks aggregating only $400—say $300 in A's favor and $100 in B's favor; F draws checks for

$100 in C's favor, and $100 in D's favor. The next day all of the checks come together at the Clearing House, and all of the transactions which gave rise to the drawing and depositing of all of the checks are settled by the payment into the Clearing House of $700 by A's bank, and by the receipt from the Clearing House of $100 by B's bank, $100 by C's bank, $100 by D's bank, $100 by E's bank, and $300 by F's bank. All of the transactions are not completely settled, of course, until each bank debits and credits its own customer, in accordance with the checks drawn and deposited. Now this is a fair illustration of customary redemption. If a timid receiver of a check should draw the money instead of depositing the check, he would take a step toward "ultimate redemption," but if after that he should deposit the money in another bank, he would step back again. If he should receive paper money from his bank, have this money exchanged for gold, and then hide the gold, there would be a case of "ultimate redemption." "Ultimate redemption," if it mean anything, means that people generally are going to behave in this manner. In time of panic they do behave somewhat in this way, but for many years no panic, in any great and civilized commercial country, has been sufficiently severe to lead people into going farther than one step toward "ultimate redemption"—that is to say, every demand for money has been satisfied with paper money, not a fraction-of-one-per-cent. preference being shown for gold.[1]

The illustration of Clearing-House work, above given, shows how an aggregate of $4,600 in transactions may be settled by the use of $700 in money, but the real state of affairs is far more significant, the New York Clearing-House, during the year ending October 1, 1891, having settled transactions amounting to $34,053,698,770[2] by a transfer of balances of $1,584,635,499,[3] this being less than one-twentieth part of the greater total. Suppose "ultimate redemption" to seize the inhabitants of New York City, the average bank clearings amounting to $111,651,471 per day, and

---

[1] Gold commanded a fractional premium in 1895.
[2] Figures for 1895 are, $28,264,379,126.
[3] Figures for 1895 are, $1,396,574,349.

you have all the gold, silver, and paper in the country in their hands in about a fortnight! True, gold and silver together would last more days than would gold alone, but the difference is not important.

If from the transactions of a city we turn to the transactions of the world, this moonshine of "ultimate redemption" becomes still more clear. Theoretically we pay, in gold, for whatever we buy in foreign countries: practically, we send out of the country gold to the extent of less than one tenth of the sum of our merchandise imports. Theoretically, we receive gold for all the merchandise that goes out of the country: practically, we receive gold to the extent of about one thirtieth of the sum of our exports of merchandise. And if there were a record of the movements of securities, much smaller fractions would have to be used to show the relation of gold movements to the sum of merchandise and security movements. In London, the Clearing House of the world, our exports are set off against our imports, and every day there is an adjustment of differences, a settlement of balances. Other commercial countries are always, too, adjusting balances at the same place. Imagine the magnitude of the world's volume of trade, and you will see that $8,000,000,000 of "real money" for such a purpose as "ultimate redemption" would go but little farther than $3,727,000,000 of gold. Neither sum would do, and certainly that portion of either sum which the power of all trading nations, using all their forces, could collect for the purpose of "ultimate redemption" at any place or at any time would be insignificant when compared to the volume of business to be settled.

We must look upon redemption in practice not as it may be in dreams. Every day in the year, paper promises are being redeemed and new paper promises are being issued, and continuous redemption and continuous issue will go on, keeping pace with each other, everybody taking part as he can or as he sees fit. The sum of money in use in the world fairly well suits the business needs of the world, in the practical conduct of such business, the redemption that goes on all the time being the only possible kind of redemption. And if the world use less silver for the purpose than it should use, in order to comply with the Senator's views, that is the fault of silver or the fault of the Senator's views, not the fault of the world. People sell goods for checks, drafts, notes, etc., but have in mind the using of their receipts in the purchase of goods, the loaning of capital, or in the making of investments; to hold actual money or to keep a large sum credited at the bank meaning to lose interest. Assisted by financial facilities, always growing, extending, and improving, the world's trade and commerce have gone on increasing and expanding, and on the whole the world is doing fairly well, and nobody need be troubled long by the theory of "ultimate redemption."

NOTE.—Of late years there has been economical progress even in the matter of bank credits or balances in bank. Clearing-house systems have been so extended that many transactions in stocks and merchandise which used to call for separate settlements are now nearly offset by each other, checks being needed only for resultant differences.

CHAPTER XII.

THE OLD VOLUME-OF-MONEY THEORY.

The theory that variations in prices and in industrial activities are due often or generally to variations in the volume of money, is so persistent that the hourly, daily, weekly, and yearly denial of this theory by the movements of prices, on the floor of every commercial or stock exchange in the world, does not suffice for a complete overthrow. In early life, we notice that the more money we have the more things we can buy, and the higher the prices which we can afford to pay. We place money and things in two opposing positions, money struggling to advance everything, while everything naturally tries to sink to a low level; and so when prices move upward or business is active we think that the supply of money is plentiful, and when prices move downward or business is dull we say that money is scarce. It does not appear to be important that hardly ever are movements in prices or changes in industrial activity accompanied by changes in the volume of money, nor does it affect the life of this old theory to show that a downfall in prices has occurred while the volume of money has been increasing! The theory is bred in our bones and will live on!

During the past twenty years or so the prices of commodities in this country have fallen to the extent of an average of about thirty per cent., and business has been alternately slow and brisk, and brisk and slow, but, concurrent with this decline in prices and this undulatory movement of trade, there has been an increase in the volume of money, in circulation, to the extent of about ninety-four per cent., being an increase, *per capita* of population, of about twenty per cent., as shown by the following tables furnished by the Director of the Mint, Mr. H. O. Leech, to the Committee of the House on Coinage, Weights, and Measures, 1891.

"The following tables [page 186] exhibit the comparative amounts of the various kinds of money in actual circulation at different periods. The various sums stated in the tables are all exclusive of money in the Treasury. They represent, as nearly as is possible, the exact amounts of the several kinds of money in actual circulation among the people at the periods named."

Accompanying the increase in volume of money and in sum *per capita,* and emphasizing the truth that money has not been really scarce, there have been a fall in the average rate of interest, an advance in the average rate of wages, an advance in rents, and an advance in the price of real estate. But in spite of all this the silver advocate points to the fall in the price of silver bullion, talks of the "demonetization" of 1873, and reiterates the exploded volume-of-money theory, without stopping to consider that we now have a greater volume of money and more money, *per capita,* than ever before in the history of this country.

The erroneous notions of our day are similar to those which prevailed in the first

TABLE No. 1.—*Comparative statement showing the changes in circulation during twenty years from October 1, 1870, to October 1, 1890.*

	In circulation October 1, 1870.	In circulation October 1, 1890.	Decrease.	Increase.
Gold coin	$78,985,305.00	$386,939,723.00	.	$307,954,418.00
Standard silver dollars	.	62,132,454.00	.	62,132,454.00
Subsidiary silver and fractional currency	38,988,995.00	56,311,846.00	.	17,322,851.00
Gold certificates	28,511,000.00	158,104,739.00	.	129,591,739.00
Silver certificates	.	309,321,207.00	.	309,321,207.00
Treasury notes, Act July 14, 1890	.	7,106,500.00	.	7,106,500.00
United States notes	329,489,221.00	340,905,726.00	.	11,416,505.00
National bank notes	294,337,479.00	177,250,514.00	$117,086,965.00	.
Total	770,312,000.00	1,498,072,709.00	117,086,965.00	844,847,674.00
Net increase				$727,760,709
Circulation per capita in 1870				$19.97
Average net increase per month				$3,032,336
Circulation per capita in 1890				$23.96

TABLE No. 2.—*Comparative statement showing the changes in circulation during ten years, from October 1, 1880, to October 1, 1890.*

	In circulation October 1, 1880.	In circulation October 1, 1890.	Decrease.	Increase.
Gold coin	$261,320,920.00	$386,939,723.00	.	$125,618,803.00
Standard silver dollars	22,914,075.00	62,132,454.00	.	39,218,379.00
Subsidiary silver	48,368,543.00	56,311,846.00	.	7,943,303.00
Gold certificates	7,480,100.00	158,104,739.00	.	150,624,639.00
Silver certificates	12,203,191.00	309,321,207.00	.	297,118,016.00
Treasury notes, Act July 14, 1890	.	7,106,500.00	.	7,106,500.00
United States notes	329,417,403.00	340,905,726.00	.	11,488,323.00
National bank notes	340,329,453.00	177,250,514.00	$163,078,939.00	.
Total	1,022,033,685.00	1,498,072,709.00	163,078,939.00	639,117,963.00
Net increase				$476,039,024
Circulation per capita in 1880				$20.37
Average net increase per month				$3,966,992.00
Circulation per capita in 1890				$23.96

half of the century, and which Thomas Tooke refuted by a life-long record of price-variations. He proved that prices obey natural laws and only follow monetary changes in exceptional cases, prices often moving, indeed, in the direction contrary to that which known monetary changes would indicate. Mr. Tooke's work is now so rare that I think it not out of place to quote from him, in order to show how closely the logic of a half-century ago, in England, fits the circumstances of the present time, in America. Mr. Tooke's *History of Prices* covers the period from 1793 to 1856. I quote from vol. ii., p 267 :

"But whenever a fall of prices since 1819 has taken place, if there happens to have been coincidentally any actual or supposed reduction of the amount of the circulation, such is the prevalence of the currency theory, that the proceedings of the Bank (Bank of England) are usually referred to as the moving cause of the alteration of prices. Thus the money crisis, as it is called, of the latter part of 1836[1] is, in

[1] Foreshadowing our panic of 1837.

most of the circulars of that period, assumed to have been the cause of the fall of prices in those instances in which a fall did occur, while in the instances of the large classes of articles which experienced either no fall, or none worth mentioning, and some indeed of the most important of which had coincidentally risen in price, the more peculiar circumstances affecting them are held to be sufficient to account for their not coming under the influence of the currency.

"There was, in fact, nothing like an extreme general depression of prices during the severest pressure of the money market, before the end of November, 1836. The greatest fall that occurred in that year was in the article of tea. But it is well known that the importation was on a scale of unprecedented magnitude. . . .

"The following articles, embracing the largest amount of value, experienced no fall, and the greater proportion actually rose, in price coincidentally with the pressure on the money market till the close of 1836.

"Corn, meat, butter, Irish provisions and

bacon, oil, tallow, hemp, iron, copper, dyewoods, rum, besides many minor articles, were as high in November, 1836, as in the spring of that year, and the greater part of them higher. And, inasmuch as those that had fallen were in no degree more depressed than the difference of actual or approaching fresh supplies warranted, the inference that such fall was directly caused by the state of the money market in the summer and autumn of 1836 is not legitimately drawn.

"So prevalent is the theory of the paramount influence of the currency, that most of the writers of commercial price-currents and circulars are infected by it." Mr. Tooke copies one of the price-currents, published at the close of 1836, reviewing the commercial transactions of the year, and showing the writer to be fully imbued with the currency, or volume-of-money, theory. Then, says Mr. Tooke: "The whimsical part is that, in giving a succinct account of the variations of each of the articles, the decline of those which fell in price after the spring and summer of 1836 is rationally explained by circumstances *quite indepen-*

dent of the state of the money market." Concluding his remarks upon this fair specimen of price-currents of those days, Mr. Tooke adds: "The reasoning here is exactly that of the currency doctrine; the articles that fell in price are supposed to have been exclusively under the influence of the contraction of the Bank issues, which, by the way, had not then been contracted in any degree worth mentioning; while those articles that had not fallen, or were rising, are stated to have been under the influence of local or peculiar circumstances."

In Mr. Tooke's time a contraction of the Bank issues, whether the contraction had actually happened or not, was charged with putting down the prices of some commodities, such commodities, for instance, as had declined in price because of over-supply; and the supposed contraction was supposed to have had no effect upon the prices of those articles which had not declined in price. In our time "Demonetization," although there has been no demonetization, and contraction of the volume of money, although there has been no contraction, are charged with putting down the prices of commodities, and no importance is attached to the circumstances that interest has declined, that real estate has advanced, and that wages have gone up—no importance whatever to the most important of all considerations: the reduction in the prices of most commodities and the advance in wages, together, have placed the major portion of our population in a better position than ever before attained.

No more consistent are these volume-of-money theorists when they cite France as an example of a country which has a proper volume of money. Did the having of forty-four dollars *per capita* lead the people of France into the attempt to control the copper output of the world, or into the attempt to dig the Panama Canal, and is the loss of hundreds of millions in these ways the proof that it is better to have forty-four dollars *per capita* than to have, as we do, only twenty-four dollars *per capita?*[1] And

[1] The report of the Secretary of the Treasury, Mr. Carlisle, 1895, estimates a decrease in circulation between Nov. 1, 1894, and Nov. 1, 1895, from $1,672,093,422 to $1,598,859,316, or, say, $24.27 per capita to $22.72 per capita.

if we are able to go into "wild-cat" speculations upon a capital of only twenty-four dollars a head, our ventures being often "wilder" than French ventures, what right have we to envy the French? At least it is incumbent upon these theorists to show that business is more brisk in France than it is in America, that farmers over there find it easier to get along, that wages are higher, etc., etc., for if all this cannot be shown—and everybody knows that it cannot,—then it naturally follows that, in this respect, the currency theory fails. As a matter of fact, does it not appear that the people of France use forty-four dollars each without deriving any benefit from so excessive use of money? By the ordinary standards, I should say that the people of France are worse off than the people of America, and in spite of the truth that Frenchmen have, individually, say about twice as much money as we have. There is here no paradox though, unless we forget that wealth and money are not synonymous. Different nations use different volumes of money and different sums *per capita*, somewhat in proportion to wealth possessed, but more in inverse ratio to the development of banking facilities and largely in accordance with the habits of the people. The amount of money in France *per capita* is very much larger than it is in the United States, but no person would say that the wealth in France is greater *per capita* than in the United States, that wages are higher, or workmen better employed, or that business over there is more active than it is here. Frenchmen keep money in old stockings; we put it in banks. The banking system of France is in a comparatively simple state,[1] ours is highly developed. The "silverites'" just cause for complaint, therefore, if they have any just cause for complaint, is against the American people for their habit of parting with money as soon as they get it. If we could be taught to carry always a few pounds of silver in our pockets the silver in use in this country would be largely increased. Or, if we could be shown the advantage of

---

[1] *The Theory and History of Banking*, by Charles F. Dunbar. Chapter on the Bank of France.

hiding either silver or its paper representative under the floor or putting it anywhere but in bank, where it immediately begins to do about ten times the amount of work naturally expected of it, the circulating medium would have to be much larger than it is. The "silverites" should find fault also with the people of Great Britain, as their habit of banking their money instead of hoarding or handling it, is quite as objectionable (?) as our own; Englishmen leaving to take care of itself to a great extent the need of an increased supply of money to match the increase in wealth, in business, or even in population.[1]

A great deal of money may circulate in a country without producing any of the results which theorists of the currency type would expect—good business, low interest, high prices, high wages, etc. Business may be unsatisfactory or the reverse, the rates of interest at financial centres may vary between one per cent. a day and one per cent. a year, prices and wages or either of them may be high or low, and we can

[1] The circulation of money in the United Kingdom, notwithstanding the immeasurable greatness of the volume of business transactions, is equivalent only to about $18.60 *per cap*.

assert that within reasonable limits any state of affairs may exist coincidentally with a large or a small volume of money. In truth, this country has experienced many conditions of trade during the past decade or two, while the volume of money has been advancing.

It is argued that money is the base of credit, and therefore the more money we have in circulation the greater can be the expansion of credit; on the contrary, however, wealth in general is the actual base of credit, and money is only a small portion of the total sum of wealth. Excepting in time of panic no one thinks of handling money in a large way. No prices are higher for cash than for check. Nobody refuses credit to a customer because that customer has stocks, bonds, merchandise, real estate, instead of money in his pockets. Nearly all the time prices move up and down for causes which directly affect commodities, individually or in groups.

In time of panic there is always an appearance of a scarcity of money, due to the circumstance that for a short time money is compelled to do a great deal of the work which ordinarily is done by credit. Money is unsuitable for about nine tenths of the work of modern business, and if there were twice as much money in circulation the character of money would not be changed. The work must be done by credit or the volume of exchanges be enormously reduced. Usually, therefore, the remedy for a panic is not the issuing of new money but the doing of something to restore confidence, which remedy may be, or may not be, the issuing of new money. In the panic of 1890,[1] the banks of New York settled many of their daily claims upon each other by using Clearing-House certificates, instead of money, and thus bridged over the time when money appeared to be scarce, or the time when money was forced to do more work than it ought to do. A temporary form of credit was adopted; and this served also as an example to business men, the restoration of the use of credit among them being the proper way to bring business back into the only channel which can hold it. No student of human nature and of the history of finance will think that

[1] Also in 1893.

panics or periods of business depression can be prevented; or that panics and periods of depression cannot occur or have not occurred under any monetary system, or in any country using any volume of money. A panic may be the natural culmination of a trade movement, and generally a panic *does not mean* that more money is needed in circulation, for, after a panic, money usually becomes apparently over-plentiful. A *temporary* expedient is, I think, the proper remedy for a panic, although whenever a panic occurs there is sure to be heard the money-scarcity complaint.

Temporary substitutes for money (such as Clearing-House certificates) have this advantage over real money: When money becomes over-plentiful, after a panic, these substitutes may be quickly cancelled, whereas real money would remain in circulation and would tend to make gold leave the country.

Abandoning the volume-of-money theory, we necessarily give up using *the rate of wages*, *the average of prices*, *the rate of interest*, and *the state of trade* as *perfect* tests of the volume of money in circulation, as to whether the volume be at any particular time too large or too small; but, however erratic have been the movements of trade, of prices, and of the rate of interest during the past twenty years, while the volume of money has been advancing, still the average of prices, the rate of interest, the rate of wages, and the state of trade must be taken into consideration, with all facts and circumstances, if we are to ascertain what volume of money is best suited to us. A good step in the right direction, I think, is the striking out, as irrelevant, the fact that Frenchmen use the equivalent of $44 dollars each; and with this fact, another, that the East can get along with about $4 *per capita*, for we have to do with American conditions only.

Now, what tests have we? One country uses the equivalent of $44 *per capita*, another say $4 *per capita*, others any sum between; but no country is a proper example for us. And if we take our own experience only, we find that within ten or twenty years, judging by all the tests I have named, we must have used at times twice or thrice as much money as we ought to use, and at other times only a small fraction of the sum which we ought to have used; but, of course, we are forced to these absurd conclusions by our failure to constantly bear in mind the *naturalness* of the *undulatory* character of trade, price, wage, and interest movements. If, however, we look upon these movements as necessarily undulatory (see explanation in Chapter II.), and then bring another element into consideration, *the rate of foreign exchange,* we shall have a fair chance to ascertain, approximately, what volume of money is best suited to the interests of this country.

Fortunately, there is no need for trying to construct a pure theory. We can assume that our habits and our business methods are correct, and that the volume of money which we actually use is somewhere near the proper volume; but this means nothing in regard to the quality of the money and to the proportion of each kind to the other kinds, for arbitrary laws, rather than natural development, have determined quality and proportion. And while, therefore, it is hard to say whether all the interests of this country could be better served by a smaller or by a larger volume of money, it need not be at all difficult to show that the interests of this country would be better served by a better quality of money. I think it perfectly clear indeed, that if we had had different currency or coinage laws, we might easily have accumulated gold instead of a large portion of the silver which we have accumulated. In other words, if our legislators had paid less attention to the demands of "silverites," of cheap-money demagogues, and of volume-of-money theorists, and had given due study to the subject of *foreign exchange*, these legislators might have been able to see the wisdom of allowing our *production of gold* to do its share toward augmenting our total circulation. The volume of money in circulation might now be as great as it is, and the composition of the circulation might be much better if there had been in our currency and our silver laws provisions for the suspension of silver purchases and the suspension of the issue of paper money, *whenever gold was being exported.* If it be the duty of Congress to provide a suitable volume of money, it is no less a duty to provide as good money as possible; but, on the contrary, it would seem that the majority had conceived their duties to be: first, take care of our silver-mining industry; secondly, provide plenty of paper money; thirdly, *supply American gold to the rest of the world.*

The author has no space here for showing the desirability of *elasticity* in the volume of money; and, he has not wished to belittle the importance of the country's having a properly large volume of money. He has tried to show the importance of the proportion of our kinds of money, and to bring out the truth, that demands for new issues of money are generally ill-founded; and, certainly, ought to go unheeded whenever compliance with such demands must result, not in augmenting the volume of money, but in displacing the best money by inferior money.

CHAPTER XIII.

SUPPLEMENTAL.—A RETROSPECT.—THE PANIC OF 1893. — REVENUE DEFICIENCY. — FINANCIAL FLOUNDERING.—BOND-ISSUING.—PAPER MONEY REDUNDANCY.—THE CIRCULATION.—BI-METALLISM.—THE FINANCIAL SITUATION IN 1896.—THE ELECTION.—CONCLUSION.

The original concluding chapter of this work was written in 1892, and was directed particularly against the Silver Purchase Law. The objectionable clause of that law was repealed November 1, 1893, after a great crisis had brought home to the masses of our people the vital financial question, and had taught them that all other national questions were comparatively unimportant. Given a proper revenue for the Government, the question, for instance, whether duties should be raised or should be lowered, concerns few persons directly and materially; but financial revulsion may shake the great industrial structure of our land to its very foundations.

How far the business of the country has retrograded in activity since the panic of 1893 may be shown by a comparison of the totals of bank clearings for the United States, commencing with the period of three months just before the panic, and ending with the first quarter of 1896:

VOLUME OF BANK CLEARINGS.

1st quarter,	1893	$15,647,000,000
"	1894	10,377,000,000
"	1895	11,165,000,000
"	1896	12,117,000,000

In the period, 1893-1896, the general financial question has been closely connected with the Government revenue question. Of course, no such decline in trade as that indicated by the decline in volume of bank clearings could take place without seriously reducing the revenue of the Government, for when people economize they do not discriminate in favor of dutiable goods. Quite naturally the income of the Government fell below the expenditure, and in spite of a reduction in the expenditure itself. For the fiscal year, ending June 30, 1893, the income of the Government was $2,341,000 in excess of the expenditure; but ever since the income has been deficient, say, by $69,803,000 for the year ending June 30, 1894; by $42,805,000 for the year ending June 30, 1895; and by about $26,000,000 for the year ending June 30, 1896. In order to avoid a consideration here of the effect on the revenue of tariff changes, I will add that the McKinley Law was superseded by the Wilson Law on August 28, 1894, and I shall gladly permit the reader to charge the deficiency to legislative action, to the decline in trade, or to both, my necessity being simply to call attention to the deficiency and its bearing upon governmental finance.

In connection with these figures we may note that for two years they seem to have been very surprising to the Secretary of the Treasury. In his annual report, dated December 19, 1893, he forecast a deficiency for the fiscal year, then current, of $28,000,000, which proved to be $41,800,000 below the actual deficiency. On December 3, 1894, he made a better guess by estimating the then current year's deficiency at only $22,800,000 below the figure which proved to be the real deficiency. On December 10, 1895, however, it is fair to add, he more closely estimated the probable deficiency for the current fiscal year ending June 30, 1896. I suppose that the Secretary's miscalculations are somewhat responsible for the financial floundering of the Administration in 1894 and 1895, the first two sales of bonds not being commensurate with the needs of the Government to cover revenue deficiency and to provide for the growing demand for gold in exchange for greenbacks, this demand increasing with the growth of sentiment, just or unjust, that the Administration had not mastered the situation.

The period of trade depression commenced with what was called a "Currency Famine," the summer of 1893 being distinguished for the peculiar state of financial affairs, in which money itself was bought and sold, payment for it being made by checks drawn on banks, which checks were not cashable, but were " good through the Clearing House." If you had a balance to your credit in a bank, that bank would certify your check, and with it you could buy, say, 96 per cent. to 99 per cent. as much money. It was a time of almost universal bank suspension, considered technical rather than real—a period when necessity overrode law and custom. With equal disregard of law and custom, there came into existence, in the summer of 1893, many substitutes for money, mainly issued by employers of labor to pay off their hands, these substitutes being good at local stores and redeemable by the issuers with checks, good in turn through the Clearing House or aggregations of local banks.[1]

I trust that no reader of this work will be astonished to learn that such a currency famine could possibly occur just when the volume of circulation had reached its highest point, for it should be clear that no volume of circulation, however large, can satisfy the wants of trade when general distrust causes traders to ask for money instead of checks, or causes even a small portion of the community to hoard money rather than to put it into banks. The Treasury Report for April 1, 1893, gives the following figures of circulation, which may be compared with those of earlier dates on page 186:

---

[1] See Hon. John De Witt Warner in Sound Currency for Feb. 15, 1895, published by New York Reform Club.

Statement showing the amounts of Gold and Silver Coins and Certificates, United States Notes, and National Bank Notes in circulation April 1, 1893.

	General Stock, Coined or Issued.	In Treasury.	Amount in Circulation April 1, 1893.
Gold Coin	$546,673,424 00	$138,874,473 00	$407,799,951 00
Standard Silver Dollars	419,047,305 00	359,490,115 00	59,557,190 00
Subsidiary Silver	77,197,330 00	11,165,155 00	66,032,175 00
Gold Certificates	116,621,439 00	5,135,430 00	111,486,009 00
Silver Certificates	328,226,504 00	5,267,551 00	322,958,953 00
Treasury Notes, Act July 14, 1890	135,490,148 00	6,533,367 00	128,956,781 00
United States Notes	346,681,016 00	29,887,702 00	316,793,314 00
Currency Certificates, Act June 8, 1872	17,090,000 00	420,000 00	16,670,000 00
National Bank Notes	176,094,544 00	3,827,111 00	172,267,433 00
Totals	2,163,121,710 00	530,600,904 00	1,602,521,806 00

Population of the United States April 1, 1893, estimated at 66,587,000; circulation per capita, $24.07.

The circulating medium had not been decreased in volume, but the amount of money held by banks early in 1893 was down to the "apprehension point," as will appear by comparing the figures below.

Money held by New York Clearing House Banks[1] on or about April 1st:

1892.	1893.	1894.	1895.	1896.
$150,129,800.	$120,495,600.	$219,422,000.	$139,135,000.	$137,454,000.

Money held by New York Clearing House Banks in excess of the legally required 25 per cent. reserve:

1892.	1893.	1894.	1895.	1896.
$18,017,900.	$10,663,000.	$80,797,000.	$13,929,000.	$17,005,000.

Trade had been brisk in 1892, and was good in 1893, until employers found difficulty in obtaining money with which to cover the weekly pay-roll. Immediately some employers commenced the practice of keeping money in strong-boxes, to have it handy, and some banks avoided, so far as possible, the paying out of cash. It is a well-known principle in finance that depositors leave money in banks in proportion to the supposed ease with which it can be gotten out. In 1893, depositors became hoarders, and some selfish and unpatriotic receivers of money became sellers of it instead of depositors. Banks of deposit were soon forced to curtail the usual loans to their customers; these, in turn, were

---

[1] Nearly seventy banks and eighty connected institutions.

obliged to curtail their purchases of goods; and the manufacturers of goods had to cut down the production of them, and to discharge the men who were no longer needed. The surplus reserve of the banks disappeared, and on August 12, 1893, the weekly report of the New York Clearing House banks showed that they held $16,500,000 *below* the sum required by law, the total sum in hand being only $76,500,000. To settle balances among themselves, the banks used Clearing House certificates, issued by the association against securities, and thus economized in the use of money to the extent of over $41,000,000.

Within a few months the process of general liquidation of loans and general checking of industrial enterprise worked ruin to thousands of business men and hardship to tens of thousands of workmen. In due course, however, the lack of use for money brought about a condition of money-glut instead of money-famine. Not only were the Clearing House certificates promptly canceled, but by February 1, 1894, the New York Clearing House banks found themselves in possession of the unwieldly sum of $249,500,000, being $111,600,000 in *excess* of the legally required reserve.

In the summer of 1893, the demand for money was greater for paper money, because of convenience in handling, than for gold or for silver; but as soon as money largely accumulated at the financial centres of the country, New York not being exceptional, an alarming preference was shown for gold, and the troubles of the Treasury grew serious. It is true that some preference had been shown for gold over other money ever since the passage of the Silver Purchase Law, the Treasury's receipts of gold certificates in July, 1890, at the port of New York,[1] being 95 per cent. of the total receipts, and thereafter diminishing until May, 1893, when no gold certificates at all were paid into the Treasury. In July, 1890, the gold in the Treasury, not represented by outstanding certificates, amounted to $184,000,000; but by April, 1893, this free gold had fallen for the first time below $100,000,000, the generally accepted danger line. The Treasury continued to lose, and in January, 1894, its free gold, amounting to only $69,700,000, it was found necessary to adopt a new policy—that of bond-issuing—for the purpose of obtaining gold with which to continue paper-money redeeming. Accordingly, $50,000,000 five per cent. ten-year bonds were sold for $58,660,917, and gold payments being exacted for the bonds, the Treasury's holding was put above the $100,000,000 line, but was found to be in March, 1894, after the bonds had been paid for, only $107,446,000, some gold having gone out even while the bulk was coming in. In about five months this free gold dwindled to $52,189,000, from which sum it was built up to $61,878,000, the

---

[1] More than two thirds of the government customs are received at New York.

banks exchanging gold for paper and showing the same public spirit which they had displayed in parting with gold for the $50,000,000 bonds not wanted at the time and on the Treasury's terms. In November, 1894, the Treasury had to be helped again, and again $50,000,000 five per cent. ten-year bonds were sold, the yield this time being $58,538,500 gold. This gold, and more, immediately flew out of the Treasury, and in February, 1895, its reserve was down to $41,340,000, and several millions of this was demanded. The bankruptcy of the Treasury, its failure to continue the paper redeeming, which was commenced in 1879, seemed imminent. Popular hoarding of gold had increased with the growth of distrust in the Government's ability to maintain gold payments. There was hoarding, too, because those who wished to buy of the then foreseen issue of bonds had to have gold with which to pay for them, the Government taking only gold in payment.

In this emergency new features were introduced —that of issuing bonds for gold coin, or ounces of gold—3,500,000 ounces—not less than half of the gold to be obtained abroad, and the bankers, entering into this contract, agreeing also to exert their influence to protect the Treasury from withdrawals of gold. Humiliating to this country of boundless resources as was this stipulation for protection, this issue of bonds was more satisfactory than the two preceding issues, for people had confidence in the ability of the bankers. Gold hoarding and gold exporting were both checked. Carrying out the terms of this bond contract, $62,315,400 four per cent. thirty-year bonds were issued for $65,-116,244 gold; and the bankers, after completing the contract, gave to the Treasury $16,-127,432 gold in exchange for paper money, the Treasury not being left to its own devices until the autumn of 1895. As late as December 10, 1895, the Secretary of the Treasury, in his annual report, wrote most enthusiastically of the results of this third bond sale:

"Confidence in our securities as safe and profitable investments was at once restored to such an extent that they ceased to be returned to our market for sale, and a very considerable demand for them was created abroad; but the most gratifying evidences of improvement in our condition were afforded by the prompt revival of business among our own people, the increased activity and extension of our domestic industrial and commercial operations, the rise in the prices of our principal agricultural products, and the general feeling of relief and security which became apparent in every part of the country. These encouraging indications of increasing prosperity still continue," etc., etc.

Alas! The Venezuelan Message of the President and its hasty endorsement by Congress were not in sight. As lightning from a clear sky, this warlike document struck the industrial and financial world just one week later. Confidence vanished; American securities were sent home for sale; the foreign demand for "Americans" disappeared; business activity gave way to stagnation, and enterprise to extreme timidity; prices fell; the loaning of money nearly ceased, for the rate on call loans was advanced to 80 per cent. per annum;[1] gold was hoarded, and gold was exported; and the New York Clearing House Association, to keep the panic within bounds, authorized its Loan Committee to assist such of the Association banks as might ask assistance. None of them happened to be in condition to need it, but the assurance that no well-managed bank would be permitted to fail was welcome to the community. The banks generally exercised great caution in lending money, and so their surplus reserve was not allowed to fall below $15,939,000, the figure reached on December 28, '95.

On the other hand, the free gold in the Treasury continued to diminish, and five or six weeks later it was down to $44,563,000. During the same period the New York banks had added to their money surplus reserve, and it had grown to $40,182,000.

At the turn of the year, bankers were ready to take the fourth issue of bonds, for some time seen to be inevitable. Two hundred millions of dollars in gold could have been obtained by the Government, but not without a profit to the bankers, on

---

[1] The New York State Usury Law does not cover large call loans secured by collateral.

re-sale or distribution of the bonds. The difference, however, between the sum which the Government would get and the sum which the bankers would receive, supposing that they could market the bonds at or near current quotations, was so great that popular clamor prevented a fourth issue of bonds on the basis of the third issue. The cost of protecting the Treasury and of keeping the rate of *foreign exchange* below the gold-exporting point and the risks involved were not appreciated by the public.

A popular loan was determined upon, and on January 6, 1896, the Government asked for bids for bonds to the extent of $100,000,000, having thirty years to run from 1895, bearing interest at the rate of four per cent. per annum, gold coin receivable in payment, and the bids to be opened thirty days later. Although the public had not wanted the first issue of bonds, it was found on opening the bids for this fourth issue that no less than $568,269,000 bonds were now wanted, nearly 4,700 separate bids having been filed, and at prices ranging upward to 119.32. The $100,000,000 bonds were awarded to the highest bidders, the yield of gold being $111,378,836. A portion of this sum was deposited in the Treasury before the bids were opened, and as soon as the loan was seen to be successful, a new era of prosperity dawned on the business community. On May first, 1896, the Treasury held $125,500,000 free gold, and the

New York Clearing House banks held $146,600,000 in money, which was $22,900,000 above the reserve required by law. The Venezuelan matter was in the hands of an investigating committee; the Cuban matter was not troublesome; and new dangers were not yet above the horizon.

President Cleveland has carried the country through the three years of revenue deficiency, amounting to about $140,000,000, and we are still upon the gold foundation. For this the largest measure of gratitude is due, and perhaps we should not indulge in criticism of the ways and means employed.

It seems to me, however, that the country might have been saved about two years of worry and anxiety, with the incalculable loss inflicted upon our industries, if, instead of a great jurist, orator, and statesman at the head of the Treasury Department, there had been a man of skillful touch, with his finger on the financial pulse of the nation. The panic of 1893 was not quite unique in its character. Inactivity in trade was sure to follow, and the Government revenue was sure to diminish even without the change in the tariff, then prospective. In the natural course of events, too, money was to accumulate at financial centres, and people who would be obliged to keep their capital in idle money, might choose to keep only gold, that being the safest kind of money. In fact, the currency was to become redundant, and the approaching financial illness was to require all the skill of the most able doctor in finance which this country can produce. But no prophet was needed late in 1893, for money had already accumulated, and a preference was already shown for gold. Yet it was not until there was widespread alarm concerning the Government's position that the first bond sale was determined upon. Then the Secretary found difficulty in getting help, even to the extent of $50,000,000 gold, although more than twice as much of the yellow metal was held by the New York Clearing House banks alone. He had waited until holders of gold felt that $50,000,000 would do little good. It might have been easier to get $100,000,000, if such a sum would be certain to suffice, and if the Secretary's own record up to that time were felt to be a sure guarantee that the country would be kept upon a gold basis, at any cost or any sacrifice; for it must be borne in mind that banks and bankers would lose by financial disturbance, incident to our slipping off the gold base, far more than they could hope to gain by selling their gold at a premium.

The law permitted the selling of bonds at not less than par in coin (gold is not named), and a later law declared it to be the established policy of the United States to maintain the two metals on a parity with each other at the ratio of 16 to 1. Of course the Government must keep its promises to pay on demand, and therefore all its money, including paper, must be kept in a state of equality in purchasing power. The national disease which appeared in the winter of 1893-1894 was that of paper-money redundancy, the true remedy for which is paper-money withdrawals. Under existing law paper money could not be canceled—it must be reissued—but it could have been drawn into the Treasury, to go out again just as gold was actually drawn in only to go out, in exchange for paper. In stipulating that bond purchasers should pay gold, the market for new bonds was first restricted to those who held gold, and then a new demand for gold was created, this demand to be satisfied by the Treasury itself. To sell $50,000,000 bonds for gold was difficult; to sell $100,000,000 or $200,000,000 bonds for any moneys bearing the Government stamp would have been easy, and the higher premium to be obtained would have amounted to many millions of dollars. A great financier in whom the world had absolute confidence might have taken the stand that every dollar of Government money must be kept upon a par with all the other dollars; that creditors of the Government must be paid in the kind of Government money which they choose to take; and that debtors to the Government, whether the debts grow out of taxes or out of bond-purchasing, must be allowed to pay in the kind of Government money which such debtors choose to offer. It is the business of the Government to draw in the kind of money which the people do not choose to keep. Under no circumstance should the Government dishonor any of its promises, or admit that one or two kinds of its own money are not good enough for the Government itself to accept. Standing on such a broad platform, and announcing to the world that he would sell whatever quantity of United States bonds should prove to be necessary to cure the existing disease, the right man would have received the assistance of the whole community; and there can be no doubt that a sufficient portion of the payments for bonds would have been made with gold.

It would have been seen at once that bond-selling could be made to result in drawing money into the Treasury faster than it would go out; that the market rate of interest on loans would be advanced; and that exportations of gold could be stopped or importations induced. In 1896, when there was a greater demand for money, and less money lying idle in bank vaults, the people offered to buy five times the total of bonds which the Secretary offered to sell, and even with gold payments stipulated. In 1894, might not our people have been rightly approached, given confidence in the Treasury, and aroused to the understanding that to protect it is to protect ourselves, and to uphold it upon the gold foundation is to uphold our own structure of trade and industry?

The following table shows the condition of the Treasury on July 1, 1896, and the amount of money in general circulation:

Statement showing the amounts of Gold and Silver Coins and Certificates, United States Notes, and National Bank Notes in circulation July 1, 1896.

	General Stock, Coined or Issued.	In Treasury.	Amount in Circulation July 1, 1896.
Gold Coin	$567,931,823 00	$111,803,340 00	$456,128,483 00
Standard Silver Dollars	430,790,041 00	378,614,043 00	52,175,998 00
Subsidiary Silver	75,730,781 00	15,730,976 00	59,999,805 00
Gold Certificates	42,818,189 00	497,430 00	42,320,759 00
Silver Certificates	342,619,504 00	11,359,995 00	331,259,509 00
Treasury Notes, Act July 14, 1890	129,683,280 00	34,465,919 00	95,217,361 00
United States Notes	346,681,016 00	121,229,658 00	225,451,358 00
Currency Certificates, Act June 8, 1872	31,990,000 00	150,000 00	31,840,000 00
National Bank Notes	226,000,547 00	10,668,620 00	215,331,927 00
Totals	2,194,245,181 00	684,519,981 00	1,509,725,200 00

Population of the United States July 1, 1896, estimated at 71,390,000; circulation per capita, $21.15. Gold Bullion in Treasury, $32,217,024; Silver Bullion in Treasury, $119,053,695 (cost).

At the end of the fiscal year, the Government held about $100,000,000 free gold, as the foregoing table will show, if from the sum of gold coin held there be deducted the gold certificates outstanding, and if there be added $32,217,024 worth of gold bullion owned at that time. No general alarm was felt on account of the Treasury's reserve having again reached the $100,000,000 mark. Twenty-five million dollars in gold had gone out in the last two months; but this was in the period of ordinary annual gold exportation, just expired; and in these two months the revenue deficiency was less than $5,000,000.[1] Besides, Secretary Carlisle had earned the confidence of the people.

Comparing the figures in the above table with those in the tables of earlier dates (pp. 186, 206) the recent decline in circulation *per capita* becomes evident. As the population must continue to increase, a further decline *per capita* appears to be inevitable, unless Congress shall provide new currency. But whether *circulation per capita* shall decline or not, it is absolutely certain that if Congress will do nothing, the quantity of money in circulation must be, before long, precisely that quantity which is best suited to the wants of our people. There is room for a great improvement in the *quality* of the circulating medium, and confident prediction may be made that such improvement naturally will be made by injections of gold, if

[1] Money total owned by Government May 1, 1896, $270,000,000, including gold reserve; July 1, 1896, about $267,000,000.

simply a place be left for the yellow metal. Silver heresies and silver legislation have forced us to use the white metal and its paper representatives; have driven gold out of the land; and have cost the industries of the country thousands of millions of dollars. Now that we no longer burden our circulation with paper money, issued against purchases of silver bullion, gold is beginning to show signs of remaining here. The world's annual production of the precious metal has grown to $200,000,000, of which nearly one quarter is mined in the United States, and no country in the world is so well situated for securing its full share, for here the most enterprising and energetic people in the world are engaged in developing the greatest natural resources. Naturally our own accumulations of capital, and much of the world's accumulation, seek investment here, and it is not creditable to American common-sense that for many years investors have failed to receive proper encouragement by an assurance that an investment of good money would yield a return of good money. Nobody could foretell how far the silver heresies would prevail, nor whether a thousand dollars, worth one thousand *gold* dollars, when invested in any enterprise would be worth more than five hundred *gold* dollars when the time should arrive for reimbursement from such enterprise. Worse still has been the feeling among investors, that the possibly coming financial revulsion, incident to our slipping off the gold base, might render worthless almost any particular investment. Happily now, this country is approaching the time when a practical demonstration may be made of the theory that gold will fill any void in the circulating medium.

Stress need not be laid on the decline in circulation *per capita,* although much money is carried in people's pockets, and therefore the *per capita* circulation has to be considered. The impossibility of financial legislation, in the present state of disagreement between the branches of Government, and the fact that much time must elapse before new men can actually pass laws, give good ground for hoping that before any disturbing laws can be passed, either the influx of gold or the disappearance of the exportation habit will challenge the attention of theorists and demand an explanation. The European stock of gold is the largest ever known, amounting to the equivalent of nearly $900,000,000 in the four governmental banks of England, France, Germany, and Austria-Hungary alone. There is a plethora of gold in Europe, owing to our having foolishly chosen to use silver and silver certificates instead of gold and its representatives. But expanding trade in this country, with its usually accompanying advancing rate of interest, ought naturally soon to draw gold from Europe, or to keep our own gold here if silver heresies can be kept down. It would not be wise, however, to say that a fifth issue of Government bonds is not imminent, for the crops of 1896 are not yet assured, money is still in such small demand that gold exportation is talked of or actually taking place, and besides, those politicians who have obtained possession of the machinery of the Democratic Party are doing all they can to discourage foreign investment in American securities. On the other hand, it may be said that bond-issuing is no longer a prime factor in financial affairs, for there is no uncertainty regarding the overwhelming success of another loan if it should be offered, bonds of the last two issues, known in the market as 4s of 1925, commanding a premium of about thirteen[1] per cent. If it could be known that in case another issue of bonds shall be made, payments for them may be made by checks, the checks to be collected before the bonds are delivered, time for payments and delivery being extended over a period of several months, that no discrimination will be made against any money bearing the Government stamp, and that the only preference to be given to gold will be an allowance to cover the cost of delivery, say, about one quarter of one per cent., then prospective bond-issuing need not check any enterprise, for the public would have no inducement to draw gold from the Treasury in order to obtain the means for paying for the new bonds, the Treasury gold might not get alarmingly low, and if it did, the new loan would build up the reserve without disturbance to business.

[1] Quite recently the market price was about five per cent. higher. The decline seems to be owing to the expectancy of a new issue.

[At the moment of going to press, many of the banks of New York City are voluntarily giving gold to the Government in exchange for legal-tenders, its gold having suddenly fallen below $90,000,000. It is said that $20,000,000 gold, about one third of the bank-holdings, will be turned into the Treasury. The banks of other cities may show a similar spirit of patriotism, and the foreign-exchange bankers may assist in postponing a fifth issue of Government bonds by selling exchange to would-be exporters of gold, thus enabling them to obtain gold in London, the bankers' opportunity for reimbursement occurring when cotton and other crops move across the ocean.]

The Election of 1896 will afford the opportunity to kill and deeply bury our enormously expensive notions regarding silver, general discussion having shown the cuttle-fish expediency of the word bi-metallism and having forced politicians out into the open, where each may be known to be either for the Gold Standard or for the Silver Standard. The currency of no country in the world rests practically upon a bi-metallic base, and every country which has not restricted its silver coinage has reached, necessarily, the silver base and has lost its gold. Bi-metallism became useless for campaign purposes. Happily, too, Protection is laid aside, although of course those who believe in it may continue to believe in it.

The important plank of the Republican Platform is as follows:

"The Republican party is unreservedly for sound money. It caused the enactment of the law providing for the resumption of specie payments in 1879; since then every dollar has been as good as gold.

"We are unalterably opposed to every measure calculated to debase our currency or impair the credit of our country. We are therefore opposed to the free coinage of silver, except by international agreement with the leading commercial nations of the world, which we pledge ourselves to promote, and, until such agreement can be obtained, the existing gold standard must be preserved. All our silver and paper currency must be maintained at parity with gold, and we favor all measures designed to maintain inviolably the obligations of the United States, and all our money, whether coin or paper, at the present standard, the standard of the most enlightened nations of the earth."

The pledge to promote an international agreement in favor of the free-coinage of silver is puerile, for no important nation will enter into any such agreement with us, nor will argument show that a general agreement is desirable, although wholly impracticable. International conferences, however, are harmless, and, in view of their educational uses, we may ignore this point, and gladly accept the Platform and commend its builders for placing the party in the position of upholding the honor and the credit of the country.

The important plank of the Democratic Platform is as follows:

"RECOGNIZING THAT THE MONEY QUESTION IS PARAMOUNT TO ALL OTHERS AT THIS TIME, WE INVITE ATTENTION TO THE FACT THAT THE CONSTITUTION NAMES SILVER AND GOLD TOGETHER AS THE MONEY METALS OF THE UNITED STATES, AND THAT THE FIRST COINAGE LAW PASSED BY CONGRESS UNDER THE CONSTITUTION MADE THE SILVER DOLLAR THE MONEY UNIT AND ADMITTED GOLD TO FREE COINAGE AT A RATIO BASED UPON THE SILVER DOLLAR UNIT.

"WE DECLARE THAT THE ACT OF 1873, DEMONETIZING SILVER, WITHOUT THE KNOWLEDGE OR APPROVAL OF THE AMERICAN PEOPLE, HAS RESULTED IN THE APPRECIATION OF GOLD AND A CORRESPONDING FALL IN THE PRICES OF COMMODITIES PRODUCED BY THE PEOPLE, A HEAVY INCREASE IN THE BURDEN OF TAXATION AND OF ALL DEBTS, PUBLIC AND PRIVATE; THE ENRICHMENT OF THE MONEY-LENDING CLASS AT HOME AND ABROAD, THE PROSTRATION OF INDUSTRY AND IMPOVERISHMENT OF THE PEOPLE.

"WE ARE UNALTERABLY OPPOSED TO MONOMETALLISM, WHICH HAS LOCKED FAST THE PROSperity of an industrial people in the paralysis of hard times. Gold mono-metallism is a British policy, and its adoption has brought other nations into financial servitude to London. It is not only un-American, but anti-American, and it can be fastened on the United States only by the stifling of that spirit and love of liberty which proclaimed our political independence in 1776 and won it in the war of the Revolution.

"We demand the free and unlimited coinage of both silver and gold at the present legal ratio of 16 to 1, without waiting for the aid or consent of any other nation. We demand that the standard silver dollar shall be a full legal tender, equally with gold, for all debts, public and private, and we favor such legislation as will prevent for the future the demonetization of any kind of legal money by private contract."

The thanks of the nation are due to the Democratic Party for recognizing that the money question is paramount at this time. The reference to the Constitution and to the coinage under it is misleading; and it is difficult to understand what is meant by the British policy of gold mono-metallism. England, by not permitting the issue of notes below £5—about $25, equivalent—forces Englishmen to carry much silver, and apparently it has never occurred to Englishmen that India might be brought into more certain financial servitude if India should be ordered to give up using silver. It is true that it would not suit English, French or German investors in American enterprises to have us adopt the policy of free-silver coinage, and if its adoption were probable, both foreign and domestic investors would try to sell out. Investors, however, do not control governments; and those foreign governments or governmental banks which have been nearly as foolish as we in accumulating vast quantities of silver, might be pleased to see free-coinage adopted here, because we should then furnish both a good market for silver and a good supply of gold. Still, the plank may be welcomed as a clear declaration for that policy of free-silver coinage which leads inevitably to the silver-monometallic base for all our moneys; that policy which would enable a few peculiarly situated debtors to defraud their creditors to the extent of about fifty per cent.; that policy which means industrial paralysis, business failures, lack of work, and national dishonor.

The friends of the white metal would be able to make out a better case if the acts of governments could properly be called "demonetization" acts; if such acts had not been forced upon governments by the natural decline in the market price of silver bullion; if the decline in the prices of commodities were due to such acts instead of to natural causes;

if the decline since 1872 in the prices of commodities were a bad thing for the vast majority of people; if the producers of silver were better entitled to governmental favor than the producers of wheat or cotton; if most of the years since 1873 had not been years of unparalleled industrial growth and development; if the average rate of wages had not advanced, in spite of declining prices; if the proportion of unemployed persons had become unusually large; if money-scarcity were now indicated (?) by an average high rate of interest; if there were actually a "debtor class;" if an important number of debtors could possibly be benefited by free coinage; if there were any conceivable way by which the Government could make money plentiful in poor and sparsely populated regions; if the sums of money which Americans want to use in trade and want to carry in their pockets could be increased by act of Congress; if Gresham's economic law had never been discovered; if no disposition to export gold had been shown; if any country in the world had succeeded in its efforts to make gold and silver circulate together under free-coinage laws; if free coinage of silver would not certainly demonetize gold; if those dead American statesmen who are quoted in favor of bi-metallism had lived to favor it after silver had become cheap and plentiful; if, in the evolution of the world's trade and industry, silver had not been rejected and gold had not been selected, in the most natural manner possible; if wage-earners, salary-earners, pensioners, savings-bank depositors, and life-insurance beneficiaries ought not be paid in the best kind of money; or if, by following the lead of any other if, we should find any invulnerable argument in support of the silver theory. There is no such argument, and the duty of the hour is to annihilate the plausible assertions which are put forth by silver advocates.

The capture of the Democratic Party by the advocates of silver did not put up the market price of this metal, and did not cause a great panic among investors; but because the financial world shows no apprehension of Democratic success at the polls, it must not be felt that there is really no ground whatever for such apprehension. Great armies, over-confident and cursed by inertia, have been beaten by small armies active and enthusiastic.

Every cause but the cause of Sound Money under the Gold Standard has been cast aside. To merely win in such a struggle would be disgraceful, because the good name of our country, at home and abroad, is at stake. People all over the world have purchased American bonds and stocks—national, state, municipal, corporate, private—with the understanding that when the time should arrive for selling or for redemption, our legal money would be as valuable as it was at the time the purchases were made. Over and over again, in legislation and by public statements, have we given investors good ground for such an understanding; and particularly it is true of our Government bonds that, without such an understanding, they could not have been sold. Shall it be said that within about two years our Government has received over $290,000,000 gold under false pretences?

Ever since the first of January, 1879, business enterprise in this country has depended in large measure for its assistance from American and foreign owners of money, upon the assurance that all our moneys would be kept upon an equal footing. Profits have been earned and salaries and wages have been paid to the extent of many millions of dollars in excess of what could have been earned and paid if capitalists, instead of lending, had hoarded their money in the belief that when the American people should get a chance to cheat them it would seize the opportunity.

Wage-earners and salary-earners are now in receipt of weekly or monthly sums, with which certain quantities of goods may be obtained. The Silver Party sees a way to advance the prices of these goods, but sees no way to advance wages in order that the wage-earner shall be able to live as well as he lives now. On the contrary, the Silver Party proposes to bring about a financial crash, which would paralyze trade and industry, and throw millions of men out of employment. When business got used to new conditions, and borrowers again should be able to borrow, prices are to advance, and presumably wages are to limp after, but starting from a new and very low level.

Pensioners have been allowed good money; savings-bank depositors have placed good money in banks; life-insurance beneficiaries are entitled to as good money as was paid to the companies in premiums. But the Silver Party sees no injustice in trying simply to put up the prices of goods, failing to see that all people whose incomes are now fixed by law or contract would, if obliged to pay high prices, be cut off from much of their usual supply of the necessities and luxuries of life. A certain sum of money would buy a smaller quantity of goods at high prices than now at low prices.

It is not enough to carry the presidential election only. Tremendous efforts must be made to carry as many congressional districts as possible. The Senate of the United States stands for Silver, and is likely to so stand during the life of the next House of Representatives. The election must make this branch of the Government overwhelmingly in favor of the Gold Standard. The formation of a tariff-silver combination by an important number of the members of both houses of Congress must be rendered absolutely impracticable.

Prosperity waits for the assurance of Sound Money. Profit-earners, salary-earners, wage-earners would do well to forego a portion of their present income to insure their future income. Pensioners, savings-bank depositors, and life-insurance beneficiaries should help in the struggle to keep the value of money up to the present level. Every good citizen, not excepting any of the wise and solvent debtors, should be willing to take time from his usual pursuits to settle forever the silver question. No sacrifice is too great to make certain the crushing defeat of the Silver Party, to protect our national honor, to uphold the American people's reputation for honesty, and to obtain the lasting assurance that every American political party of the future shall inscribe upon its banner Sound Money and Honest Finance.

INDEX.

American, business **ways**, 199; business expressions, 27, 28; borrowing, 132–134; common sense, 174–220; conditions, only, 198; dollars, equality of, **216**; preference for paper money, 3, 19, 20; securities, 126, 127, 131, 135; silver, 147, 148; travelers, 128
Atkinson, Mr. Edward, 16, 29, 86, 87
Austria–Hungary, 170, 221

Balance of trade, 114, 115
Bank clearings, 179, 180; **203**
Banking and currency measures, 226
Banking, evolution of, 9–11; English, 5, 194; facilities, 161; **French, 196**
Bank, of England, 5, 16, 187, 221, of France, 151–154, 193, note, **221**
Bartine, Hon. Horace F., 72–76, 154, 172, 173
Beck, Mr. William H., 80–83
Bi-metallism, 223
Bland, Hon. Richard P., 154, 166, 171–174
Bond-selling, 209, 213, **222**; bond premium, **222**
British Royal Commission, 33, 38
Bullion-value dislocation, 38
Business, assumptions, 95, 99; growth, **161, 181, 182; sayings, 27, 28, 38,** 93; ways, 177–182; American, 199
Buyer, a very good, 148, 149, 155, 156
Buyers and sellers, 62–66

Carlisle, Secretary, 219
Campaign against silver theories, 223
Capital, timidity of, 111, 138; foreign, **132**, 135, 143
China, 18, 20, 22, 35, 47, 56, 58, 163
Circulation, general, 221; reduction from pro-silver legislation, **165;** tables, 186, 206, 218; late decrease, 219
Circulation, per capita, 184–186, 191, note, 206, 218, 219, 227; in France, 191–193; in the East, 198; in the United Kingdom, 194, note.
Civilization, financial tests of, 18–21
Clearing House, 16; certificates, 196, 197, 208; work, 177–180, 196, 197; New York, transactions, 179, 180; the world's, 5, 180, 181
Cleveland, President, 214
Coinage-parity or ratio of silver to gold, 150–154, 159–162
Coins, 41, 50
Colorado, 81
Committee of House on Coinage, Weights, **and** Measures, Fifty-first Congress, 5, 29, note, 58, 66–72, 75, 168–173, **184**
Commodities, cost of production, 40, 44
Comstock miners, 73, 74
Congress, duty of, 21, **22, 31**
Confidence, 211
Copper, 3, 157
Corn, English meaning of **word, 25, note**
Coup de Finance, 154
Credit, base of, 195

Index.

Creditors or debtors? 101-113
Cuba, 47
Currency famine, 204
Currency theories, 48

Debtors, corporations, 104; farmers and planters, 105; governments, 103 merchants, 104; no "debtor class," 106; individual, injured by laws intended to benefit, 109-113; dishonest (?), 112; **debtors or creditors?** 101-113
Democratic Platform, 225
Denver, 77
Depression, 68, 78, **202**
"Dislocation," 40, **41**
Dollars, American, equality of all, 216; **Mexican, 54**
Dunbar, Prof. Charles F., 193, note

Election of 1896, 223
Employers, 65
Engineering and Mining Journal, New York, iv., **72, 73, 76, 77**, 160
England, 5, 20, 39, 221
English habit, 194
Europe, 4, 163, 221
Evening Post, New York, 116, note
Evening Telegram, New York, 144, note, 150, 158

Farmers, 31, 33, 37, 38, 49, 83, 84, **table, 89-91, 104, 192**
Financial contrivances, 16-18, 205
Financial floundering, 204
Financiers, 10
First Principles, 24
Foreign Exchange, 52, 55, 58, 115, 116; balance of indebtedness, 121-124; "favorable" trade, 116-121; guide to legislators, 143; inferences to **be drawn from** rate of, 129-131; movements of securities, 121-124; par of exchange, 115; rate of, a **test** of the circulating medium, 199-201; rate of interest, 128
Foster, Sec. of Treas., 56
France, 4, 20, 89; Bank of, 151-154, 193, note, 221; circulation **per capita**, 191-193
Free-coinage, 157, note; see Silver; trying it for **a year, 155**
Freight remittances, 125

Gaul, a wily, **154**
Germany, 4, 20, 89, 221
Gold, accumulating, 221; American production, 220; circulation, **186**; certificates, **186**; demand for, 164, 165; demonetization, 5, 42; English need for, **5**; exportation, 121, 128, 130, 131, 137, 149, 151-155, 201; how to supply Europe, 165; importation, 121, 130, 131, 137; little used in business, 21; misuse in Europe, 20; movements of, 115-119, 180, 181; premium, 143; production, 128, 160, 200, 220; **proper base of** value, 3; stability of, 6, 8, 21, 22; supplying foreigners with, 201; supply of, 221; unsuitable for small coinage, 3; **unsuitable** for hand-to-hand use, 3
Gold Hill, 73, 76
Goschen, Right Hon. George J., M.P., 115, note
Governmental safeguards, 15, 16; embarrassment, 209, 215
Greenback retirement, 227
Gresham's Law, 4, 142
Grier, Mr. John A., 30, 39

H., Mr., 144, 145, 147, 148
Happy Community, 73
History of American Currency, 2

Index.

History of Prices, 187-191
Holland, 163
Homer, 1
Horton, Mr. S. Dana, 39, **note**

Ifs and ifs, 225
Increase in circulating medium, 184-186, 191, note
Indebtedness, balance of, 121; character of, 134; **to foreigners, 121-124**
India, 18, 20, 22, 35, 36, 45-47, 49-61, 163
Industrial Progress of the Nation, 86
Industries, American, 89-100; European, 89-92; **development of, 44-48**
Interest and dividends, 125, 128
International, conferences **and agreements, 31, 39; movements of securities, 121-124**
Inventions **and discoveries, 44**
Investors, 220
Italy, 92

Japan, 22, 163
Joke, a, at our expense, 149
Jones, Mr. John P., 73-75

Labor-saving inventions and machinery, 40, **44, 88-100**
Labor organizations, 67, 68
Leech, Hon. E. O., Director of the Mint, **168-173, 184**
Life-insurance beneficiaries, 113
Lippincott's Magazine, iv., 30, **37**
London, World's Clearing-House, 5, 180, 181

Manning, late Secretary, 30, **32, 38, 39**
McKinley Law, 203
Mexican dollars, 54; silver, 147
Mexico, 22, 35, 163
Mint, operation, 173
Monetary changes, 39, **44**, 48; dislocation, 31, 32, **38**, 40
Money, accumulation at financial centres, 208; and prices, 183, 184; cheap, 101-113; Confederate, 57; demands for more, 201; displacement of best, 201; erroneous notions, 185-187; evolution of, 1-3, 7, 12; glut, 208; hoarding, 207; how used in trade, 177-182; kinds in circulation, 186, 206, 218, table; limited demand for, 162; not appreciated in value, 50; or Wealth? 162, 195; Oriental, 54; paper, 12-16, 57, 201; plentiful, 140, 141; proportion of kinds, 199-201; quantity of gold and silver in the world, 175; relative positions of the metals, 3; held by Clearing-House banks, 207, 208, 212, **214**; tables of circulation, 186, 206, 218; temporary substitutes, **196**, 197, 205; volume increasing, prices falling, 184, 185
Mono-metallism, 35
Montana, 80

National bank notes, 186, 206, 218
New Granada, 45
Newlands, Hon. Francis G., 83
New processes, 44-48
Nottingham Guardian, 22, **note**

OK, 58
Oriental bankers, 61; consumers, 51-55; exporters, 51-55; ignorance, 19; importers, 51-55; moneys, 19, 54; people, 19; producers, 51-55; use of money, 19; wages, 19
Our special partners, 139

Index.

Panics, 71, 77, 187, note, 195–197
Panic of 1893, 203, 207, 208
Pensioners, 113
Political parties, 223; political platforms, 223, 224
Popular loan, 213
Price-currents, 187–190
Prices of commodities, decline in, 29–36, **43**, 50, 65, 78, 83, **84**; benefit of the decline, 45–48, 62, 79, 86, 87; decline not affecting wages, 72; naturalness of the decline, 38, 40, 42–48, 93, 95–99; undulatory movement of prices, 23–29, 199
Production of gold and silver, 160, table
Prosperity, 69–79, 86–88, 99, 100, 223
Pueblo, 77
Pugh, Senator, **154**

Quinine, 45, 46, note

Recent Economic Changes, 23, 38, 42
Redemption, 209; customary, 177–182; "ultimate," 175–177
Redundancy, 214
Republican Platform, **224**
R**e**serve, 164
Revenue, 202
R**e**venue deficiency, 203, 204, 214
Rupee, 49–61; actual value, 49, note; nominal value, 49, **note**
Russia, 58

Savings banks, 102, 113
Secretary of the Treasury, 204
Securities, description of, 126, 127; **fear of influx**; 131; **movements of,** 121–124, 135–140
Seignorage, 157, note
Senate, 224
Silver, Act of July 14, 1890, 149, 202; advocates, 62, 185; American, 147, **148**; Am. view, 6; ctfs., 186, 206, 218; circulation, 186, 206, 218; coinage, **30**; profit on, 166, 167; coins, 3, 41, 50; cost of producing, 80–82; "demonetization," 29, 31, 36, 40–42, 68, 100, 159, 185; educating up to silver standard, 163; enforced circulation, 20; European policy, **4**, 20, 163, 164, 170, 171; evolution, 2–5; exportation, 149; fear of pro-silver legislation, 135–140; no benefit to come from, 109–112; free coinage, iv., 145–149, 150–155, 163–167; the equivalent of unlimited purchase, 165–174; governmental action, 4, 31, 45, 100, 102, 113, 157, 163, 201; hoarding, v., 60, 61, 74, 75; heresies, 220; importation, 145–154; improvements in mining, 80–82; in Bank of France, 151–154; instability, 21, 22; in 1873, 70; lost caste, 8; Mexican, 147; mining industry, iv., 73–83, 147–149, 155–157, 201; wages of miners, 73, 74; mono-metallism, 35; Oriental demand, 55–57, 59; "out**lawry**," 29, 40, 41, 42; pathetic view, 5; price or value, 6, 8, 41, **43**, 60, 106, 145, 146, 150–157, 162–174; production, 4, 6, 8, 9, 76, 157, 160; **cost of,** 80–82; purchase, **iv.**, 31, 39, 145–149, 163–167, 171–173, 200; restoring (?), **33**; secondary money, **3, 8**; subsidiary, 186, 206, 218; **suitable for poor countries,** 18–20, 22; supply, 4, 145, 146, 151–154, 157, 163, 164, 170; taxing importations, 148; Treasury, the, as a market for, 164, 170; Treasury notes, 186, 206, 218, table; vital point in silver question, 65, 66; world's view, 161
Silver in Europe, **39**, **note**
Smith, Adam, 1
Société des Metaux, 157
Sound money, right of way, **227**
South **America**, 22, 46
Southern borrowing, 133
Spencer, Mr. Herbert, 24, 43, 48

Index.

Stewart, Senator, 144-146, 154, 158, 159, 161-168, 174, 175, 182; possible punishment, 146
St. John, Mr. Wm. P., 150-154
Sugar, 47
Sumner, Prof. Wm. G., 2
Supply and demand, not equal, 25

Tariff agitation, 224
Taylor, Hon. Abner, 168, 169
Tea, 47
Theory and History of Banking, 193
Theory, an exploded, 185-191, 194
Theory of the Foreign Exchanges, 115, note
Tooke, Thomas, 187-191
Trade, evolution, 1-12; expressions, 27, 28; **payments**, 177-182; undulatory movement, 24-29, 184
Treasury notes, 186, 206, 218, tables
Treasury receipts, 209
Treasury stock of gold, 206, 209, 210, 211, 212, 213, 218
Treasury protecting, 210
Treasury, Secretary of, 204, 215, 216, 217

United States notes, 186, 206, 218, tables

Vaux, Hon. Richard, 170, 171
Venezuelan panic, 211
Virginia City, 73, 76
Vital point in silver question, 65, 66
Volume of money, 14-16, 48, 141, 142, 186, 206, 218, tables, 191; increasing while prices decline, 184, 185; in different countries, 192-194; persistent theory, 183-184; tests of, 197-199

Wage-earners, 63-79, 85, table, 97, 99-103
Wages, 19, 50, 64-79, 82, 84-103, 231; advance in, 64, 65, 85; how advanced, 90-100; illustration of advance, 93-95; rate in proportion to results, 97, 98
Walker, Hon. Joseph H., 83-85, 169, 170, 173
Wampum, 2, 7, 8
Warner, Hon. John De Witt, 205
Wealth or Money (?), 162, 195; base of credit, 195
Wells, Hon. David A., 23, 24, 42, 45
Western borrowing, 133
Williams, Hon. James R., 172
Wilson Law, 203
World's philanthropist, a, 165

www.ingramcontent.com/pod-product-compliance
Lightning Source LLC
Chambersburg PA
CBHW031744230426
43669CB00007B/479